A Wild Goose
and other stories

by

Mike Wells

RB
Rossendale Books

*Cover picture: "First In" Pink-footed Geese
by Martin Ridley*
*www.martinridley.com
www.facebook.com/ridley.wildlife.art*

Also by this author:
*AS I WALK WITH SPIRIT
Hypnotherapy, Past Lives,
Healing and Spirituality*

Published 2015
ISBN: 978-1-326-02697-4

Published by Lulu Enterprises Inc.
3101 Hillsborough Street
Suite 210
Raleigh, NC 27607-5436
United States of America

Published in paperback 2016
Category: Life Story & Memoirs
Copyright Mike Wells © 2016

ISBN: 978-1-326-86924-3

COPYRIGHT and DISCLAIMER
ALL RIGHTS RESERVED. No pictures or parts of this book may be reproduced or transmitted in any form whatsoever, electronic or mechanical, including photocopying, recording or by any informational storage or retrieval system without express written, dated and signed permission from the author.

DISCLAIMER AND/OR LEGAL NOTICES: The information presented herein represents the view of the author as of the date of publication. While every attempt has been made to verify the information in this book, either the author or his affiliates or partners assume any responsibility for errors, inaccuracies or omissions. Any slights of people or organisations are unintentional. Any reference to any person or business whether living or dead is purely coincidental.
All pictures in this book belong to Mike Wells and come under copyright laws of 2016 and must not be copied or used under any circumstance without written prior permission.

Dedications

For my son Simon - Enjoy...

And to all the goose shooters, wildfowlers and everyone involved with shooting and conservation. Long may goose shooting continue for all to enjoy. Keep up the good work.

*Last, but not least, to my wife **Jaqui** for all the amazing work she's done helping me with this book - without her help it simply wouldn't have happened.*

CONTENTS

Introduction 9

How It All Started 11

My First Pink-footed Goose 14

Over Here Son, On My Head 25

Rats Paradise 30

Dave & The Dicky Bow Tie 38

Methven - The Village 43

A Desperate Call From A Farmer 56

Loch Leven - The Stalk 62

The Solway Marsh 71

The Solway Moon Flight 82

Don't Shoot The Spies 86

Widgeon On The Solway 100

Crief With A Goose Guide 108

Westmorland Wildfowlers 122

Dunning Perthshire 130

Alan - My Best Mate 139

It Could Only Happen To Me 147

The Blue Peter Hotel 155

My First Flight As A Goose Guide 163

That's No Lady 168

Palnure 175

A Shocking Morning 183

Where Do I Put My Hands? 189

Never Until After 10 pm 193

Towcett Estate 205

Seaville 214

East Fife: Five, Forfar: Four 220

Seaville Under The Moon 225

A Raging Torrent 231

The Long Arm Of The Law 239

Welcome To AOL 251

The Finale 258

A Father's Advice 264

Useful Links 266

Some of Mike's stories seem too good to be true but they actually did happen whilst chasing the impressive Pink-footed Goose and they should bring a smile to your face.

Introduction

Mike was born in Kendal in the North West of England in 1952. At the age of seventeen he became involved in Wildfowling on local marshes near Kendal, Cumbria. Cumbria was formerly known as the County of Westmorland; situated on the coast fifty miles south of the Scottish borders.

Mike writes about his journeys and exploits chasing that elusive bird which so many people now choose to pursue. The Pink-footed Goose (Anser brachyrhynchus), the Greylag Goose (Anser anser) and occasionally the Canada Goose (Branta Canadensis) would be taken but when Mike first started shooting, the Canada Goose wasn't as well established as it is today.

The Pink-footed Goose is a medium-sized goose; smaller than a mute swan but larger than a Mallard. It is pinkish grey with a dark head and neck, a pink bill tip with pink feet and legs. This species does not breed in the UK but large numbers of birds spend the winter here, arriving from their breeding grounds in Spitsbergen, Iceland and Greenland.

Numbers in England are still on the increase even after many years of shooting. They can be found in Norfolk, Morecambe Bay, the Solway (Rockliffe Marsh), Scotland and many other areas probably due to better protection for their winter roosts.

Mike's many journeys to Scotland became an obsession which would take over the winter months from mid-October until February 20th; for well over half of his life time. Latterly though, Mike become more involved in taking others out to have a shot at that much sought- after bird, enjoying teaching and watching others enjoy their experiences.

Mike, his wife Jaqui and son Simon took ownership of a small hotel in North West Scotland for many years taking out guns who wanted to shoot geese, ducks, and pheasants. They ranged from the experienced to the novice, the emphasis was always to ensure safety, bag limits and were fully aware that conservation played a large part in the future protection and growth for all to enjoy. A dream fulfilled in Mike's eyes.

Not all the stories in this book are about goose shooting but some stories should make you laugh as they will never happen again, it's utterly impossible. There are also a few very old pictures for you to enjoy; including pictures of cars that are no longer around.

How It All Started

It all started when I was about seventeen and my girlfriend's brother introduced me to a shotgun. A group of guns were going out early evening to shoot Carrion crows roosting in nearby woods; this was to help to protect the sheep during lambing season. Carrions are notorious killers during the lambing season, often plucking out newly born lambs' eyes and tongues. This was a good way of keeping the numbers of carrion crows controlled.

That evening I was given a side by side hammer gun to use; a nice looking English gun with thirty inch barrels and a double hammer action on each barrel. I had never seen a shotgun, never mind fired one but I was to be under close supervision that evening of Charlie (my girlfriend's brother). I was attracted to the idea of shooting immediately and just loved the way the gun fitted me perfectly; or so I was told. Unbeknown to me it was the only gun available that evening as no one else had a spare for me to have a go with.

It was an organised crow shoot which was authorised by the UK Ministry, a box of cartridges was also supplied as part of the crow control. There were possibly over forty people gathered that evening and we were shown where to go and where to stand in the wood ready for the crows coming in to roost at dusk. I had an expectation of what was going to happen as Charles had gone through it all with me prior to the shoot.

I can remember it like it was yesterday when that first crow came over me at about twenty yards in height. It was silhouetted by the trees and the fading light of the evening. Up went the gun and BOOM as I pulled the trigger, down it came, absolutely stone dead. I had shot my first Carrion Crow and I suppose that was the start of what was to follow in the coming years.

After a few years I became a very confident shot, winning many local clay shooting competitions and of course by this time I had acquired quite a number of shotguns. A Mossberg 5 shot pump action 3inch magnum, a ten bore side by side for wild fowling and a Laurona 3inch Magnum multi choke over/under for other shooting including clay pigeon shooting and of course goose shooting. I preferred to stay with the type of guns used mainly for wild fowling or goose shooting but rather than go into great detail about all the clay shooting I enjoyed over the years I will push forward to the wildfowling and goose shooting. A few of the stories are not goose shooting related but they could never happen again and I look back on them with very fond memories.

My First Pink-footed Goose

From the age of fifteen and after leaving school I worked in a local shoe factory in Kendal. It was then called K Shoes and every October we were given the first week off for a holiday. I was now twenty and looking forward to spending a bit of time at home. It was then that a work colleague and shooting pal invited me to spend four days with him in Scotland chasing the Pink-footed geese. It was an offer that simply couldn't be refused. For at least a week prior I did not sleep at all well, it was probably with the excitement of seeing my first ever Pink-foot.

Car packed, dog inside (Blackie), suitcases packed and enough shells to sink a flipping battleship, mainly 3 inch Remington's and Winchester BB's and a few boxes of number threes. Also packed were six full bodied goose decoys, nets, poles, seats etc. I was taking my trusted Larona 3 inch Mag with me and my 3 inch pump action as a backup. A number of changes of waterproofs were packed just in case it rained but with it being October it was nearly always pleasant weather. Poor Blackie could hardly move inside the car but he never ever complained; he would go anywhere with me, especially if shooting was involved.

We were to travel up in Steph's car as he had been before and knew the area very well. It was a bit of a bone shaker but fairly reliable. We would be staying in a little village called Errol near the Tay Estuary. I've long forgotten the lady's name where we stayed but she was truly amazing and treated us like family after losing her own son a few years prior. She only had one spare bed so I elected to sleep on the couch for the duration of our stay but there was a slight snag; she had every wall covered with clocks. 'Oh my god', there must have been over forty clocks in that small front room and most had very audible ticks; grrrr. I didn't get much sleep the first night but after that I was so tired I would have slept anywhere. One of my memories is asking her if she had a tin opener as I had forgotten mine and I needed to open a can of dog food for Blackie, get him fed and watered and put back into the car for the evening. The look she gave me was scary; she had never used a tin opener ever. I also remember the bill at the end of our visit being so very reasonable for four nights. What a lovely lady she was and she always looked forward to seeing her wildfowling boys coming in the winter months. I often think of her even after all this time, she was an absolute treasure.

The journey north in those days was very long and tiring. The M6 finished at Carlisle and then it was a long slow trek up and over Beattock heading northwards towards our final destination, Perth. The biggest problem then was getting passed the wagons safely, especially if they were in convoy. We would stop near Hamilton at the services to let Blackie stretch his legs, have a pee and for us to grab some breakfast. Then it was northwards again, passing Sterling making our way closer towards Perth and the Tay Estuary. It was always a good laugh and some of the stuff we used to talk about was, well I best not say here but Steph was a master at winding me up. I think half of the things he said were to get me more excited and it certainly worked. On the journey Steph would point out names of places like Blackford and Auchterarder, Dunning, Forteviot and how many geese would be in the area at that time, don't forget this was my first ever trip so I had to believe him, or did I? Was he winding me up yet again?

I remember laughing with Steph when our landlady told us if you're not back by nine o'clock you will not get breakfast. She was a very strict one indeed and trust me we weren't going to fall out or argue with her. What a woman she was; certainly old school.

Monday morning at six o'clock we came out of the digs and we were faced with about two inches of snow, a very severe frost had formed on top of it. As we headed towards the car it crunched underfoot making it very difficult to walk. The car windscreen was a nightmare to clear and seemed to take forever. Steph wasn't too sure if we would make it to the shore as the road was very treacherous but with some very slow and careful driving and a few slides and slithers we managed to get to the car park on the edge of the Tay Estuary. All I can remember was looking at six to seven foot tall reeds swaying in the wind in front of us and I still had no clue as to what lay hidden beyond them. Visibility was zero.

After a fumble around getting the rest of our shooting clothes on, making sure my ciggies were in the right pocket and my Pink-foot Goose caller was around my neck. Yes, I had a caller but still hadn't had a chance to use it; in fact I had not yet heard the wild Pink-foot call. Come to think of it, I still have that caller. It's priceless to me now so, NO!!! It's not for sale. It has called in many, many geese perfectly over the years and has some lovely memories attached to it. No doubt my son will inherit it one day soon.

It was follow my lead as Steph guided us through some colossal bunches of reeds to get us onto a pathway that would take us higher up the coastline to where he thought we might just get a chance at the geese. Blackie was tucked in by my side and at times I wished I had not trained him to walk to heel so tightly. Suddenly, I fell 'arse over tit' and slipped upside down into a shallow gutter well hidden by tangled, frozen grass; I had trapped the toe of my wader underneath somehow. Luckily, although my pride was dented a little, I was neither wet nor injured but we did have a good a laugh; at my expense of course. Good thing the gun was still in its slip and remained undamaged or it would have been a total disaster.

Although we were dressed for the weather we were absolutely frozen to the bone, our thermals made no difference at all. We had to keep moving to try and generate some sort of warmth.

We walked for a good fifteen minutes and then stopped for a brief time for Steph to get his bearings. Come on he said let's walk through these reeds to the sea's edge. We followed a well- worn pathway that other fowlers had probably used many, many times before. As we reached the end of the reeds!! Wow!!!! What a sight to behold in front of us. I could see for miles across the estuary to the far distant snow covered hills and looking to my left I could see in the distance the small outline of the Tay Bridge silhouetted by background lighting. It was awesome, I could now see and understand why people came here shooting, it was such a beautiful estuary.

It was now starting to break light so we decided to stay put but just edge back into the reeds very slightly to give us better camouflage; geese have very keen eyesight and any sudden movement would be easily spotted. A car horn went off in the distance and I nearly jumped out of my skin thinking it was a goose calling.

We sat and waited but heard nothing else apart from being taken totally by surprise as a pair of Curlews skimmed the reed beds, like a couple of Spitfires chasing enemy planes. Then being taken by complete surprise yet again by two swans going directly over our heads, only about eight feet above us, with that very distinctive sound of their humming wings. My heart was pounding in my mouth and to be so close and witness those amazing birds in flight was beyond words.

The wind suddenly dropped and apart from a few seagulls nothing was moving or calling. It's at times like that, your mind starts playing tricks on you. I was sure I could see a skein of geese coming right towards us then when I looked again it was the top of a few reeds bent over, right in front of my eyes about two feet away. I was so certain they were geese. Oh well, best not say anything, I remember thinking.

It got lighter and began to get a little warmer but still nothing. Steph looked baffled and assured me that the previous year there were thousands of geese. I was beginning to doubt him and wondered if I had been led on 'a wild goose chase' myself.

The sun was now well up and not a dicky bird to be seen or heard so it was decided that we should walk a bit higher to where the reed beds finished and where we should get a better view across the sands to see if any geese were still out there.

Once we had reached the end of the reeds Steph and I scoured every bit with binoculars but alas we couldn't see a thing. (I was gutted). It was now eight forty five and very sunny with not a breath of wind. I reminded Steph that breakfast was about to end. Oooops, we had completely forgotten. What now, do we stay or do we go, knowing full well we couldn't get back in time for breakfast and to be honest I didn't fancy a bollocking. It was just then that Steph seemed to freeze on the spot saying." Did you hear that? Listen." In the far distance towards the Tay Bridge we could see what looked like skeins of geese getting airborne. Oh my god, there were hundreds of geese starting to come towards us but still a few miles away. We had both put our guns back into their slips and it was a frantic rush to get them out again. Steph was running to take cover behind a very large boulder about fifty yards top side of me; I was going to stay exactly where I was behind a similar sized boulder. The distant noise was getting louder by the second and I dare not even peep to see where they were.

This was my first ever experience on Pinks and I was shaking all over and the noise is never EVER forgotten. I did manage to move slightly to see where they were and I could see hundreds maybe more like a few thousand birds coming straight towards us. The distant sky was black with them. The first birds went slightly left of me and also left of Steph so we didn't get a shot but by now the noise was becoming deafening as so many birds were nearly upon us. Two rapid shots came from Steph and as I was standing up to shoot I pulled through a bird and fired; NOTHING. A second shot on the same bird; NOTHING. I didn't even touch it and by now as you can imagine I was running on pure adrenalin. Trying to re-load as fast as I could was like watching myself in a slow motion video. More came right over me so I pulled through yet again, two more shots and again, nothing. Steph had shot two Pinks and shouted at me to give a lot more lead. There were birds everywhere so I waited until one skein came right over me, only about 30 yards up. Once again I stood up and selected a bird, gave a lot more lead and missed again with two shots. Now I was getting cheesed off. What the hell am I doing wrong? I'd heard a few more shots come from Steph but I hadn't been watching so I didn't know if he had shot anymore geese; I had enough to deal with myself. All those shots and nothing to show for it, I was devastated and of course just a tad embarrassed; I just couldn't understand what I was doing wrong.

Many of the birds were setting their wings and dropping into the fields behind us. Just like a parachutist coming into land after jumping out of a plane. To see them gliding in, with their wings set, was a WOW factor, so graceful and elegant. From the left of us they came, from the right of us they came but no longer coming right over us. For my first ever time seeing this unbelievable spectacle of literally thousands of Pink-footed geese and to experience the clamber and noise Wink,Wink,Wink,Wink of those birds will be imprinted in my mind until my death.

I was no longer facing forwards but leaning with my back on the boulder just watching the geese coming over me, far too high to shoot, joining their friends, hundreds upon hundreds. I had managed to light a cigarette but I was still shaking all over and trying to hold my cup of tea steady was totally impossible. I was now suffering with 'Goose Fever'. I think I was so fed up with missing four lots of what I thought were easy birds. I was completely baffled by how I had missed every time. Maybe I was giving them too much lead, I just didn't know. Steph came down to sit with me and he was carrying two Pinks. This was the first time I had ever seen one. After a bit of a breather he said he would go back and sit a bit longer and as he was walking back he shouted loudly. "MORE ARE COMING", get down! He ran like hell to get back into his hiding place and I was soon loaded and ready again, still shaking from my first encounter with the geese.

As they flew over me I once again stood up and fired two shots without a single feather being touched. Another skein came very slightly to my right, again I stood up and selected the front bird and pulled way in front of it and pulled the trigger. Immediately the fourth bird back in the line collapsed, stone dead in flight. I didn't get a second shot off as I watched my first ever Pink-foot hit the sand at such a force it split its chest wide open. I suddenly realised the amount of lead needed or should I just speed up my swing. But I was like a 'pig in the proverbial sh…' I had shot my first ever Pink-footed Goose. That's the one you will always remember. Even typing this is just like my being there and re-living it all over again and that was over forty years ago. Amazing or what?

I can hold that goose totally responsible for what happened to me for all the years that followed. I certainly had got goose fever and even Blackie my Labrador loved it. His head was continually homing in on every Wink, Wink and the rattles of wings above us.

We went back to our digs with our tail between our legs and told our landlady that it would probably be better for us all if we got our own breakfast elsewhere after we had finished shooting as it would be impossible to stick to any sort of time frame. She was absolutely fine with it and we breathed a sigh of relief. Well, it would be actually better for her as she would not have to cook for us.

A little later after a good breakfast locally it was decided that we would go and see if we could get permission on a farm inland and hopefully get a shot at the geese. We drove around the local countryside for what seemed like hours following skein after skein of geese. Finally, we found a farm where lots of geese were feeding and after a very brief chat with the owner he gave his permission for us to shoot the geese the next morning. He told us that many, many birds had arrived and they were devastating and fouling his fields. They had also brought down the nearby electric cables which meant the farm had no power at all. The electricity board had told him, in no uncertain terms, that they would not repair the electricity lines until the geese had gone back home because it would just keep on happening again and again. So I think he was only too pleased that someone was going to scare them off his land. That happened quite a lot in those days and it was great knowing we always had shooting to go to.

Over Here Son, On My Head

The next morning we awoke to just a touch of frost so it wasn't too bad but travelling in the dark was strange as we struggled to find the farm where we had been given permission to shoot. No Sat Navs or IPhones in those days. Things always seem easier in the daytime but trust me in the early morning and when its pitch black it's a totally different story. Plus, it was the first time either of us had been into that area; it was like the blind leading the blind. At least we were in good time as I was up early after listening to those bloody wall clocks ticking all night long and on top of that there was the noise of the geese from the previous morning flight still ringing in my ears. It was sheer bliss; NOT.

That morning we had a little wind but not enough to make flighting geese into the decoys any easier. We placed the hide next to a gateway and had a rough idea where the previous geese had come from and in which direction they would probably come into us. It didn't take that long to get set up as we only had six full bodied pink decoys and three dead ones. They were set up on forked sticks to look as realistic as

A Wild Goose Chase

possible. So it was a nice warm coffee, a bit of a chill and chat before there would be any sort of movement.

As it broke light geese were coming off a local loch just a few miles away and were going in all different directions to their feeding grounds but nothing was coming towards us. It's still a sight well worth watching and again it's the sound of their excitement as they get ready for a good feed after a nights rest. It's absolutely magic to witness. Don't forget I am talking about forty years ago when there weren't many people shooting geese in that area so we had the pick of a number of places where we could go and shoot. Well that's if we were given permission, most farmers did allow it though. The only time we didn't get permission was when it was a large keepered estate; this meant it was also a pheasant shoot. Not a chance of goose shooting but we did meet a few brilliant keepers who used to let us go back in spring/summer and shoot the woodpigeons and rabbits.

It was now getting later in the morning, the sun was beginning to break through and we were wondering if the previous days geese had maybe just dropped in for a quick feed before returning to the loch to roost. We had a few come over us but very high and they were shouting loudly, obviously going elsewhere. I responded on my caller when all of a sudden they started spiralling out of the sky heading straight for us, dropping like lead balloons, spinning and

A Wild Goose Chase

spiralling. I took one out in front of me at about thirty yards and it collapsed stone dead in flight. It came hurtling straight towards Steph who had his gun raised and was about to take a bird when he shouted. "Over here son, on my head" and moved his head/shoulders quickly out of its way. It hit the wooden gate stoop next to him with such force it would have killed him or certainly put him into hospital. "Bloody hell Steph", I shouted," what the heck was that; you wanted to head it or what"? Silly beggar. It must have brushed the side of his face as it passed him at great speed; he was very lucky indeed not to end up in A&E.

The geese were now moving and we did manage to get two more but a lot of the birds were seeing something and just kept flaring off. It may have been Blackie because it was a nightmare trying to keep him down as he got so damned excited when hearing and seeing the geese. I think he was also suffering with goose fever. We tried everything but they weren't having it so we decided to call it a day, get the hell out of it and go and get some breakfast in Perth.

We always went back after breakfast to thank the farmers and drop off a bottle of Grouse whisky for him and a box of chocolates for his wife. In those days we never had to pay for any goose shooting but we were always very polite, thanked the farmer and left a thank you gift. We always received the same reply, come back at any time lads. I always made a note of their contact details and would call back on them for years. As we came to know them better we would take them some shoes from the K shoe factory where we both worked. We were allowed a very good discount on a certain number of pairs per year, it actually worked out cheaper than whisky and they loved the shoes. One even called me when he knew we were going up shooting and asked if we could get him a pair of size nine K brogues which we did manage to get for him.

We made many farmer friends over the years and even sent Christmas cards to each other every year. I think at one stage after four years of going up to Scotland, sometimes four times a year and at times possibly more we accumulated a list of over twenty plus farmers we could call on at any time to shoot geese. It was brilliant being able to call them prior and see if any geese were feeding on their land. It cut out all that guess work and also saved on fuel; no more chasing geese around the area in the car.

One year while we were staying in a local hotel in Methven and even before we had chance to get changed into our shooting gear we had three calls from local farmers all wanting geese shifting. The jungle drums had already started to work. Doubt that would ever happen now; well, we know it wouldn't, that's how manic it could become at times when we were there.

The one thing we never did was abuse the geese. We did get some good large bags but always made sure they would be used; and there were only so many geese we could get in the car.

Rats Paradise

One particular farm we used to visit regularly was situated in the bottom of the valley at Forteviot, just a few miles outside of Perth. It would get thousands of geese visiting every year and was that good we didn't really need to go anywhere else to realise our dreams of Goose shooting.

The owner was a bit of a whisky head and would charge us one bottle of whisky per gun per day but even that was cheap for the quality of shooting we would get in return. The farm could take four guns easily but as many as eight guns would be possible because of its vast acreage. It was always a full car of four shooters for that visit and a good few days of first class goose shooting. However, sometimes one car wouldn't be feasible so we would go up in two cars. We then had plenty of room for the guns, decoys, dogs, nets and extra clothes etc. To travel in one car would mean we were very restricted on how many geese we would be able to bring back home with us.

On entering the farm yard there was a small concrete lane which was partly hidden by the farm itself. The lane went across the middle of the farmer's land to a very large barn where he stored most of his straw bales. Why, I have no idea because the only living animals he kept on his farm were Saddle Back pigs and they were close to the farm itself; apparently he was an expert on them. All the fields were contracted out to large whisky companies, one being 'Dewar's' so by the time we arrived the harvest was all done and dusted. Some of the fields where we shot would be in the region of fifty plus acres in size and more was left around the edges after they had finished combining than we ploughed in down in England.

On that particular trip there were three of us so we travelled in my car. The weather was absolutely perfect for goose shooting and we were looking forward to some excellent morning flighting. We never shot any evening flights because it was far too easy at times to get the amount of birds we wanted. Plus keeping them for four days wouldn't be so easy, especially if the temperatures increased.

There was nothing worse than carrying geese in the boot of the car, going down a country lane and hitting pot holes, bumps etc. and the gas coming out of the birds. All we would get was. Is that you? You dirty bugger. The geese always got the blame but at times I wasn't sure because it could have been the amount of alcohol we had drunk the previous night or maybe it could have been the take away curry from Perth. But whatever or whoever it was, it wasn't pleasant. We had the windows wide open with our heads hanging out, gagging and trying to get some fresh air. It's funny looking back, no one ever owned up to it but there was always a lot of laughter and banter.

On our arrival at the barn it was a scramble to unpack all the gear we had taken with us. At last the car was looking more like a car and not a tank on manoeuvres and the suspension heaved a massive sigh of relief when everything was removed.

With it being an open fronted barn, without doors, it was easy to conceal the car as it was simply reversed inside. Every year we would have suitcases or hold-all bags with fresh clothes to change into before going into town to get a meal after the days shooting. Looking back over the years we rarely changed choosing to remain in our shooting clothes for most of the time, just not being arsed to get changed. By the end of four days I bet we stunk and our underwear, well I'm saying no more, probably peeled off once we were home and discarded never to see the light of day ever again.

It was early afternoon so we travelled into Perth for a take away meal and decided that once we had eaten we would go to the pub which was very close to where we were staying. It was managed by a South African guy who we had known for over three years and as soon as we entered he would shout. Here's them bloody Sassenachs again from England coming to drain my pub. I think at times he may have been right as we always over indulged. Don't forget it was a holiday as well as a shooting break. And in those days there were no breathalysers or local police chasing you. If I remember rightly, I'm sure the local bobby used to have a drink with us because it was a bar tucked well out of the way; no one bothered you at all.

The landlord had probably the most flavours of crisps I have ever seen before in any pub and I think over the years we must have tried everyone. After some of our days shooting his wife would organise evening meals for us all and we always spent a small fortune at the pub but we were on holiday and money was no object. Because of its location the pub wasn't known to many tourists, it was mainly frequented by the locals who soon got to know us and used to tell us where to go and who to see for better quality goose shooting.

One of the gamekeepers who regularly drank in the pub invited two of us back to shoot pigeons in the springtime when they planted the wheat/oats and barley. It was stacked out with pigeons and we always had a great time with him. We used to meet our pub pals on regular return visits and find out where there were more farms we were likely to get permission to shoot pigeons. Some of the pigeon bags went into the hundreds and a local game dealer used to come daily and collect them in his refrigerated vehicle; he always left with a big smile on his face. The money we made from the pigeons went to the keeper; this was our way of thanking him for some fantastic shooting. I know we used to take about a thousand cartridges with us and sometimes we did run out and would have to nip into Perth to buy more shells.

We would also get chances at shooting rabbits if it was the right time of year. One day the keeper took us to look at a few fields and showed us the numbers of rabbits they had. 'Oh, my, god', when he beeped his horn the field literally, got up and ran away. I've never seen anything like it since and I doubt I will see anything like it ever again.

The estate had three keepers and their wages were subsidised heavily by the money the rabbits and pigeons brought in to the estate; it was always a pleasure helping them out. I think one night whilst standing in the back of his Subaru pick-up we shot over 100 rabbits in a few hours. It was manic with the .22 rifle and silencers just taking them as fast as we could. I've never repeated anything like that and again doubt I ever will.

Anyway back to the story, after a quite long night in the pub we made our way back to the barn. We had already pulled out a few hay bales and put our sleeping bags down ready to settle in for the night. I think it was one of the driest and most comfortable places that we had been in for a few years and we didn't have to travel far or pay high hotel prices. It was during the night that the dogs started barking loudly and woke us up. They were getting frantic about something. I fumbled around for my torch to find out what all the fuss was about.

Shock, horror, crawling over our sleeping bags were a great number of rats and I do mean a great number. I've never seen three hung-over men trying to get out of their sleeping bags so flipping fast in my life. Try finding a zip in the dark with rats crawling all over us; it wasn't easy. It scared the s...t out of us and they were massive rats, of course they had to be. (Wink) The rest of that night we slept in the car and that's how the barn got the name 'Rats Paradise'. Would we dare to go back in there again? Well we did but didn't sleep very well.

We spent three days shooting on that farm and we really didn't need to go elsewhere because of the amount of geese that came into the fields every morning. We were well and truly spoiled by the numbers of geese on that farm. We would never take big bags and once we had shot a dozen we would get the hell off the field as quickly as we could and leave the other geese to settle back in again for the next morning's shooting. We would leave our hides' in-situ and just take the decoys and dead birds back to the barn. The picture below shows the result after a few days shooting. My car then was an Austin Maxi; its seats all folded down flat into a very comfortable bed.

Mike the author at Forteviot

One of the greatest things about shooting was the mornings watching the geese as they started to lift and fly towards us from a very large nearby loch. The loch was probably three to four miles away from us, slightly to our left and on higher ground. The sight was amazing with very clear visibility, probably because we were lower down in the Forteviot valley itself. The flight could last for up to an hour with thousands of birds looking for somewhere close to land and feed. Skein upon skein lined up in the sky as far as you could see, they just filled all the air space, literally. After that flight ended geese would begin coming from the Tay Estuary, roughly about nine to nine thirty; they normally come towards us in one big mass, sometimes in their thousands. Once again there would be that familiar adrenalin rush, the sheer numbers and noise of calling Pink-feet, would make every hair stand on end. The sheer excitement of it all just willing the birds to come into our well placed decoys.

The one thing I've always loved about all the different forms of shooting I've been involved in is being able to see the many dawns and sunsets. The townies have no idea what they're missing, they really don't. Every child should be brought up with a good understanding of this fantastic country we live in and be taught about shooting, hunting and conservation. They should be taught to enjoy and look after the countryside. They should be taught that some animals need to be culled to give nature the balance it needs to survive and remain healthy. I get really angry when shooters are called murderers. We do more for conservation than the everyday person.

Dave & the Dicky Bow Tie

Dave was a very good friend of mine and we used to go shooting quite regularly up to Scotland chasing the geese. One night he asked me if he could shoot a Roe Buck and if I would mount the head for him; I was an amateur taxidermist at that time.

I had permission to shoot a medium sized fir wood which was the home of about six Roe Deer. One of the older bucks could be taken out to let a younger buck come through but getting it would not be straightforward. There was no easy way to get the buck as it was a medium sized wood of about six acres in size and surrounded by grass fields, so getting close would be difficult. Using a shooting tower wasn't an option as the wood was very thick with no suitable areas to shoot from. I suggested he use his shotgun and SG's or LG's; they were allowed in those days but getting him close enough to shoot would be very difficult, maybe even impossible.

It was planned in every detail, with military precision. Dave would have to walk quietly across two fields, go around the bottom right corner of the wood staying in the field and then walk quietly up the side until he came to a gap in the wall about three quarters of the way up. The deer would always break out at that point and make their way across to the other woodland at least three fields away.

Dave was a big guy and for those who remember Giant Haystacks the wrestler, well Dave looked like his brother, big beard and all. Plus he was a little bit short-sighted or was it long sighted. Hmm was I doing the right thing here? I just wasn't sure and maybe I should have given it a bit more thought.

As soon as Dave was in place I would walk slowly through the wood with my dogs and gently get the deer to move out. The last thing I wanted was to spook the deer and for them to go at full tilt, it just wouldn't be feasible and probably a little dangerous. Dave had his orders and he had to comply with them; he knew exactly which deer he had to shoot. If in doubt don't shoot, it was that simple. I sat and watched him walk slowly across the fields. He followed my instructions perfectly and went around the bottom right corner. I would give him at least ten minutes to reach the gap in the wall before setting off with my dogs.

I was just about to start walking when there was an almighty BOOM and a single shot echoed around the nearby hills. "What the hell has he done now" I remember thinking and I was starting to panic more than a little. This big shape suddenly appeared at the bottom corner of the wood and was running back to me at full speed, 'smoke coming off his wellies', obviously it was Dave but what the hell had he done now.

That mountain of a man was running at full speed across the fields towards me so I set off and rushed to meet him.

As he got to me he was gasping and couldn't get his breath. I asked him what the hell had happened and as he started to calm down he tried his best to explain to me between gasps. He had done as planned and went round the bottom of the wood and as he was walking very quietly towards the wall gap he saw the deer inside the wood, they were only about twenty yards from him. All six of them could be seen clearly, the one he was to shoot was standing sideways on to him but he'd had a double take and as he looked again he saw it was wearing a green dicky bow tie. You can imagine my reaction. I think it was something like what the hell are you on about Dave, what did you shoot at and what green dicky bow tie? Holy hell, what have you done I asked him again?

Within a few minutes he was starting to look as white as a sheet and he took me through what had happened more

A Wild Goose Chase

clearly and in much more detail. He told me again that when he went around the corner of the wood, slowly making his way up to the gap in the wall he heard something, so he stopped turned to his left, it was then he saw all the deer. He stood motionless for a few moments and could see clearly the one he had to shoot and it would be a clear shot but as he looked again he could see a large green dicky bow tie fastened around its neck. By now I was shouting at him, "So what did you do?" He replied, "I aimed and shot it in the neck but it ran off'. So I thought I best get back to you and get the dogs to go and look for it.

I was off like a rocket and told him to stay put while I went and looked for it. I rounded the corner of the wood and about 30 yards further on, I found his empty cartridge case lying in the grass. I lifted both dogs over the fence, got over myself and went into the wood. It wasn't long before one of the dogs let me know she had found something. She was stood still and barking into a big heap of brashings. As I went towards her I could see the white target of a Roe deer's backside and lying dead amongst the brashings was the deer Dave had shot at. It had just fallen over after he had shot it, it must have been killed outright; this made me feel a lot easier. I had imagined the wrong deer being shot and possibly wounded and having to look for it with the dogs. Pheww, what a relief!!

I slung the deer over my shoulders and carried it back to Dave; his face lit up when he saw it. His first question was "Where is the dicky bow tie?" In its mouth was a small stick with a green leaf on each end; the green dicky bow tie Dave had seen. Thank you Dave for scaring the life out of me, maybe you should have gone to 'Spec Savers'.

I still laugh about that incident now after all these years but at the time he certainly put me into a right old panic but he did get his trophy; mounted by yours truly. Job sorted but the moral to this story is, NEVER go shooting with someone who is short or was it long sighted. (Smiles)

Methven - The Village

I had been going up to Scotland with pals for years but my work position had now changed and I was making my living as a Dry Stone Waller which included barn conversions and new builds etc. I'd had to leave the K shoe factory a few years earlier because my lungs were reacting badly to the leather dust. It could have meant the normal October holidays were no longer available but now being self-employed I could pick and choose my dates. This was just brilliant for me as a goose shooter and it couldn't have worked out better.

In the previous chapter I related the story about Dave and the deer with the green dicky bow tie. Well Dave also wanted to go to Scotland to have a shot at the geese and because I regularly worked with him on building contracts we arranged a few days away. I contacted a farm and was told they had plenty of geese coming in.

Methven is a small village situated between Perth and Crief and the hotel in the village was called the Methven Arms

Hotel. Beside it was a lane that led to the farm and which could easily be missed by anyone not knowing it existed.

The farm where we were going was one I had been going to for quite a number of years and I knew the owners very well. The farmer was a tenant and had to be careful who he let on to shoot the geese; his farm was part of a very large estate. Although there were three keepers on the estate, goose shooting wasn't a priority, there were no woods just acres of stubble fields. The estate didn't have a problem with family members of the farmer shooting and we were never bothered as Mrs Donaldson always referred to us as family for years and she always looked forward to us going to see them. I think in all the times we shot there, there was only ever one call from one of the keepers asking if her boys were out shooting. She replied, "Yes. It's just my boys shooting a few geese for Christmas"(She camouflaged the truth very well indeed)

The first time I shot on their farm was at least five years earlier and I remember the very first time I met them. I asked for permission to shoot the geese and asked if we could sleep in their barn as we were roughing it for a few days while on holiday. Her response was one of shock as she replied in a very stern voice. "Indeed you will not sleep in our barn. I have two small unused Crofts so I will switch on the electric for you. It has a toilet, a cooker and running water", sheer luxury for us really; Blackie, for once wouldn't have to sleep in the back of the car. I got to know the family very well and while I was still working at the shoe factory I would take each of them a pair of shoes as a thank you for their kind hospitality and allowing us to shoot at the geese.

After a cuppa at the farm we went to the Croft and true to her word Mrs Donaldson had switched on the electric. It was small but quite cosy and soon warmed through. As we were unloading and sorting out the car geese were calling and flying over us landing on the bottom fields towards the boundary ditches. The one thing we were aware of though was it was a full moon that night and we might not get a shot at the geese but hey ho we were going to give it a try anyway.

It was just coming in dusk and the moon was up and getting brighter by the minute so the geese were taking full advantage of the extra light to feed more extensively.

Dave's face was a picture, watching, spellbound by the numbers of geese; it looked like I had had another convert in the making. (Goose Fever was setting in)

Mike with Blackie, Methven

We decided we would go for a drive into Crief and find somewhere to get a bite to eat. On our return to the Croft geese were coming over in their hundreds, maybe thousands. Once again it was very noisy, Dave was absolutely mesmerised by it all. This was his first experience hearing so many birds clambering and to see the numbers, well, his face said it all just like a rabbit startled in headlights.

I debated with myself, "Would the geese still be there in the morning, a very good possibility?" As I knew every gutter and boundary of that land, I wasn't too sure if we could get close enough to them to get a shot as we would have been spotted far too easily. It was now about one a.m. and geese were still piling into the field. How on earth would I get Dave under them when the birds were already there? It could and probably would be a total waste of time going out in the morning so I suggested that maybe we should enjoy a good rest or nip into Perth and do a bit of shopping and go out that night under the moon instead. It was agreed, it made much more sense although Dave looked a bit disappointed but the decision had been made.

I tried explaining to Dave about shooting under the moon and went through how clouds help to silhouette the birds making it easier to pick out their shapes. When it's clear all that can be heard is the wings rattling over-head but nothing can be seen. How do you explain to someone who has never experienced it before? I took him outside the Croft and we just stood watching and listening.

Because it was a cold, frosty, clear night he struggled seeing the birds but said he could hear them just above us, somewhere. Later it clouded over and it was far easier to silhouette them and see them much more clearly. He loved it and said he understood it a little bit better now. If I had taken him out without him knowing how to look for them I think it could have been a very frustrating night indeed.

Although we were warm and comfortable in our sleeping bags it was very difficult dropping off to sleep with the numbers of geese flying over the Croft; continuously shouting their heads off. I didn't care one bit but to hear it over and over again was the icing on the cake. Although

A Wild Goose Chase

Dave didn't say anything I knew he was also getting very excited. As planned we did manage to get a few hours of good quality sleep and we both felt much better for it the next morning. Although the Croft wasn't furnished we had the electric cooker to heat the place and a kettle so we could make a fresh brew and fill our flasks ready for our evenings shooting.

I took Dave outside and told him to look through the binoculars at all the geese feeding on the lower fields. I can't type what he said but I can imagine you will have a good idea of the words he used when he could see for himself the vast numbers of geese feeding. I think when he eventually spoke he asked if we could go and shoot them straight away. My reply, "as if, not a chance just be patient."

That evening we went out onto the fields around seven p.m., we'd already heard geese flying around for quite some time. It didn't take us long to get into position, the same area where the geese had been landing the previous night. The famous six full bodied decoys were placed strategically out in front of us, probably about thirty yards away from us at the most. It wasn't very long before we could hear geese flying and coming towards us. They came very low and passed over our heads, their wings rattled as they went over but we couldn't pick them out and weren't able to get a shot. More birds came and the same happened over and over again. A small bunch of about ten birds landed amongst the decoys and as they lifted we lost all visibility of them completely. It was now getting very frustrating so we decided to move. We needed some sort of background to be able to silhouette them easier. Once we had moved things improved and with cloud forming in the right places we were able pick out the flying geese. Within minutes a bunch came right into us with their wings set, gliding in like Lancaster Bombers approaching the runway. They were well in range so we got up to shoot and after four shots three geese were down stone dead. Dave's first ever shots at Pinkfeet had earned him a right and left, he was ecstatic. Within one hour we had shot around twelve birds so called it a night. It was heavy going carrying them back to the Croft with the guns and decoys but well worth it. We could still hear the birds overhead when we arrived back at the croft, the fields must have been very overcrowded by now. I suppose we could have shot many more if we had wanted to but I will never shoot more than is needed, there is simply no point. If there is one thing that really peeves me it is hearing about large numbers of geese being shot and then just being left in the hedgerows to rot; what a waste. I have had many chances where I could have shot well in excess of a hundred birds but refused. I would stop at around fifteen birds per flight and I would never take the life of a goose if it wasn't going to be utilised.

The time always seemed to go so quickly and we wanted to get in as much shooting as possible but once again we decided that we would have another evening under the moon. We washed and changed and went into the Methven Hotel which was just at the end of the lane where we turned up to the farm. We had a superb evening chatting to a few of the locals, having a few beers and a few games of pool and darts. Plus we got orders for about twenty more geese; things were looking better.

It's very rare that I spent any time in Perth city because it was normal to shoot in the morning and nip into Perth or Crief to get something to eat in the early evening. This time though it was the other way around. I was able to spend a full afternoon enjoying a bit of shopping and looking in the gun shops at guns I knew I could never afford. I even went to watch the salmon jumping at a small weir on the River Tay; it was a brilliant sight, silver salmon fresh from the sea, swimming in the river making their way upstream; an angler's dream.

Later that evening, around eight o'clock we went out to wait for the geese, concealing ourselves in a very large dyke. It was more than a bit precarious as it had very steep sloping banks and Dave being Dave, as he got up to take his shot, lost his balance and slid right down the bank into the standing water; he went down backwards losing all control. It was probably the recoil of the shot that made him lose his footing; he ended up with a very wet backside and I remember asking him if he was ok but having a chuckle to myself and trying my very best not to let him see me giggling.

The next morning we thought we would go and explore the area a bit more and it wasn't too long before we found a farm where lots of Greylags were dropping in. They were coming from every direction and piling into the field without any hesitation. I thought well, I've nothing to lose I'll go and have a chat with the farmer. After about a fifteen minute conversation he was only too pleased to let us have a go at the geese.

A very wet Dave

I got all his contact details but told him we couldn't shoot right now as it was our last day and we would be going home in the early hours of the next morning. It was left open for us to call and go back at any time. He took us for a short tour round in his Land Rover and showed us his farm boundaries. He also told us that he had quite a large loch where the geese roosted at night but it was a few miles away from the farm. What a find that was and we shot on his farm for many years after that first initial meeting. The only thing I didn't like about his farm was his sheepdog which seemed drawn to me for, whatever reason and always had a go at my blasted leg. I think you know what I mean. (Smiles) That right leg of mine was like a flipping dog magnet at times. Trying to get it off without causing it any discomfort, as I stood talking with the farmer, was a work of art; horny little bugger.

Well it was our last evening and only chance to get a few more geese so we packed the clothes we didn't need into the boot of the car. We quickly tidied the Croft, leaving it as we found it. All that we had to do before leaving the following morning was grab a cuppa, a bacon butty and then go and thank the Donaldson's, once again, for their amazing hospitality. Plus if we did get any more geese, I had arranged to drop them off at the back door of the Methven Hotel ready for the locals to collect that day. Nothing was ever wasted.

That night we went out around seven p.m. again and very much like the night before, quite a lot of geese were milling around. There was no hesitation as we went back to the same place we were the previous night and quickly set out the decoys. Quite a few birds come close but like so many times before they knew something wasn't quite right and flared off, well out of range, shouting their alarm calls to warn other birds. It can become very frustrating as many of you reading this will know and understand. We tried everything to correct it but the same thing kept on happening over and over again for over an hour.

When this happens you go through everything to try and discover the cause, is it your camo or face or are they seeing the dog, are the decoys set out right and so on. Nothing made the slightest bit of difference so we decided to move away from that field and go closer to the boundary, towards the east side of the land which was a good half mile plus away.

Again, we set out the decoys and waited and waited and waited. Nothing came near us and yet we could hear lots of birds flying over us but quite high and they weren't responding to my call at all. We were extremely fed up and cold but whilst we were sat having a coffee a small bunch of about six Pinks came and landed in amongst the decoys. Even Blackie hadn't heard or seen them which was very strange as he normally missed nothing. If you ever have any doubt, just watch your dog; they normally let you know when something is near. I whispered to Dave, "where's your gun?" He whispered back to me, "ten foot away and I daren't move in case I spook them". Well, they spooked anyway and by the time we got our guns raised they had gone and were out of sight.

We had been out for a few hours when lots more geese started coming in towards us but from a totally different direction, this could possibly give us a better chance. The sky again was lacking some cloud cover and as much as we tried to see them the more difficult it was becoming. Even Blackie had flipped a little and ran out into the field spinning around, looking up into the blackness of the night watching and trying to catch sight of the birds. He was getting very excited but it was the look he used to give me as if to say "hurry up I'm waiting." I'm sure he thought we were useless at times. It was now about two a.m. and we were becoming very cold and a frost was starting to appear on the stubble. We were thinking of calling it a night/morning, when the cloud closed in a bit more and gave us a better chance of seeing the geese.

As if by magic they came in their hundreds right over us only about twenty yards at the highest. Someone upstairs had taken pity on us and sent them. I think between us we had over thirty shots for a bag of twelve which meant our shooting wasn't particularly brilliant but talk about fast and furious. Within thirty minutes the noise of our shooting had sent the other geese packing and it went from pandemonium to total silence with just the odd call of geese being heard in the far distance.

I remember Dave saying, "Oh, my God, what the hell happened there?" He had never seen as many geese so close to him before and he had shot seven geese in that frantic thirty minutes. We sat quietly for a while and then just looked at each other with big beaming smiles. Pheww, what a moon flight it turned out to be and that nights shooting had taken us to a total of twenty-four geese, which meant a few could now be dropped off for the locals.

Dave's introduction to goose shooting had been incredible; he had loved every minute and was well and truly hooked. Another shooter with 'Goose Fever' and he couldn't wait to go again.

One of the things that always happened after returning home from Scotland and seeing and hearing thousands of geese calling continuously was the sound stayed firmly imprinted in the deepest recesses of your mind and at times I would stop, listen and think geese! Only to remind myself I was now back at home and they weren't really there, it was only my mind playing tricks again. But it's a sound that is never ever forgotten.

A Desperate Call from a Farmer

One evening I received a call from a farmer friend, I used to go and help him with pigeon control during the barley season. This was a farm on which, for many years, I'd had permission to shoot; it was also on the boundary of my friend Alan's pheasant shoot near Shap in Cumbria.

He was desperate and asked if I could go and shoot some Roe deer which were destroying his turnip field. He explained that in the early evenings they would come across from the nearby shoot, jump the fences and start eating his turnips. They were making an awful mess, even damaging a few fences. I asked if they came in a morning or through the day but he told me it was mainly early evening. I said that I would chat to the head stalker and see what could be done. I felt he would probably be the best person to take care of the problem. I contacted the stalker who told me it wasn't his land or his problem so I could do with them what I wanted; he simply wasn't interested.

I called my mate Dave once more to help me. He's the one who shot the Roe deer with the green dicky bow tie and who fell backwards into a dyke whilst goose shooting. Should I really be asking him again?

I contacted the farmer and told him that two of us would be there that following evening and asked if he wanted any venison, should we be lucky enough to shoot any deer. His reply was short and to the point. "Just get rid of those blasted things, please."

The following day, late afternoon was quite overcast with a strong south westerly wind which would be perfect and certainly in our favour for stalking. The actual forecast didn't mention much about rain so the waterproofs were left at home as we preferred silent clothing for stalking. Dave lived just outside Kendal on the A6 road which would take us to Shap village and then towards the farm. As we neared Shap there was a massive change in the weather and it was now chucking it down and to make matters worse it had sleet in amongst it. Oh no! We had left our waterproofs at home. Why I hadn't just put them in the boot of the car, I will never know?

We drove slowly towards the field just in case there were any deer, not wanting to scare them off. I will try my best to explain and give you a mental picture of what it was like. The B road was on the top side of the field and as you looked to the left the turnip field sloped down from the road for about three hundred yards. It had a grass field to the right and also to the left of it. It was totally fenced off.

We drove past very slowly and could only see one Roe standing about two hundred yards down the field and towards the centre of the turnip field. How the heck were we going to get over that wall and get down towards it without us being seen? It was starting to get darker now and we would have to make a move soon or it would be gone; the rain was now becoming very heavy, in fact it was pelting down.

We hid the car well out of the way and crawled about eighty yards up the edge of the wall and watched to see what the Roe deer was doing. Every so often it would raise its head, have a look around and then lower its head back to feed. Somehow, we had to get over the dry stone wall without it seeing us and by now we were starting to feel very wet and soggy. We made our move when the deer's head went back down; we got onto the wall lying perfectly flat and stretched out. We waited for the deer to put its head back down again to feed before we literally dropped over the wall onto the sodden grass beneath us. We were cold and wet but determined; it was a like a military exercise and done with perfect precision.

Now what we thought? We have to turn slightly to get to the fence line and somehow belly crawl well over a hundred yards to be in range for a shot. On the fence line was a slightly raised ridge of earth which definitely made it easier to keep concealed. I stretched out flat with Dave directly behind me. Before we could set off again I had to raise my head a little to see what the Roe was doing. It was still there and still feeding but I sensed it knew we were there as it kept looking towards us. It stared for a while before lowering its head again to feed. By this time and because of the amount of rain a run of fast flowing water descended on us following the fence line down the field. The fence line had turned into a small stream and the water was running up through my trousers and soaking all my upper body clothing. It was absolutely freezing and I could hear Dave's teeth chattering but we pushed on cautiously, a little bit further.

We were now on the final push, I was pleased as by now my body was extremely wet and starting to feel numb and slightly detached from me but it was going to be worth it to get a Roe deer for the freezer. Over the entire stalk we still carried the guns inside their slips, as we knew it was the safest way to carry them. They lay across our folded arms as we pushed further forwards on our bellies, only rising slightly and using our knees to push forward.

I asked Dave to stop while I took another look and sure enough the deer was still standing there. The strong wind was still in our favour so the deer had no chance of scenting us but once again it was looking straight at me and seemed to sense something or someone was there. I daren't breathe in case it saw my breath in that cold, early evening air.

We had to make our move soon or it would be over all too fast and for absolutely nothing. So turning onto our sides and getting the guns out of sodden gun slips, very, very, slowly so as not to alert the deer in any way we loaded our guns as quietly as we could. We then slithered into position ready to spring up and ambush the deer. I told Dave to shoot first and I would back him up just in case he missed.

That's it, we were ready, we both stood up and took aim; it was then we both looked at each other with surprise and burst out laughing. Our faces must have been a picture, we had successfully stalked a piece of keeper kale which had bolted and gone to seed and was blowing in the wind. It looked so much like a blasted deer. 'Should have gone to 'Spec Savers, yet again Dave' comes to mind once more. We were absolutely drenched from head to foot with freezing water running down our necks. Time for a very fast retreat and get back to the car, put the heater on and hopefully dry out a little and get warmed up. I wouldn't have minded if it was just me who had been mistaken but Dave also thought it

A Wild Goose Chase

was a deer; remembering that green dicky bow tie I should have known better. We even saw its ears moving and turning, listening. Never again would I be caught out like that and when the farmer called me the next day to ask how we got on I simply told him we hadn't seen anything but would keep an eye on things, for him. He was so grateful and would you believe it, the deer never came back to that field. Did they know something we didn't?

I know mistakes have been made with rabbits, hares etc., but a Roe Deer? I rest my case. But it's certainly given me a good chapter for the book. I personally think Dave was a jinx, on me anyway.

Loch Leven - The Stalk

A work colleague had just returned from a holiday in Scotland, he'd been staying near Loch Leven and told us that a great number of Pink-feet had arrived at the loch. We were planning another trip to Scotland so we decided to go and have a look for ourselves. We checked the map and realised it wasn't very far from where we normally went shooting. In those days there were no motorways so it was another of our exploits, driving round the countryside trying to find our way. There were no satnavs so the good old AA driver's road atlas was a godsend.

Usually, after a morning flight and breakfast we would follow skeins of geese, watching to see where they were heading. If we were lucky enough to find their feeding grounds we would then try and get permission to shoot. Whilst we were driving towards Loch Leven we could see geese everywhere, flying around and pitching into different stubble fields. It had been a few years since we had seen so many geese and looking back it gave us quite a shock to see the numbers of birds in that area.

A Wild Goose Chase

As we travelled around the loch we could see geese in virtually every field, thousands of them. We eventually found the farm and I spoke the farmer whose land went up to the edge of the loch. He was very accommodating and said he was happy to let us shoot but there would be a condition. He asked if we would give him a few hours lifting potatoes from a nearby field. After chatting to the lads we agreed and we spent that afternoon helping the farmer. 'Tatty Howking' as he called it, was absolutely back breaking, picking the potatoes up off the field, putting them into what looked like plastic washing baskets and then lifting them up and emptying into a trailer. We were well and truly knackered. There were also quite a number of gypsies helping out; in return they were allowed to take a few bits of game using their dogs but they were strictly forbidden to kill any deer.

We had a great time and such a good laugh with the gypsies, boy did they graft, they put us to shame. When we had finished we were all invited into the farmhouse for a splendid evening meal. We arranged to have a go on the geese the following morning and the farmer kindly showed us where the geese had been feeding earlier. He also showed us his private access track which would get us much closer to the loch. It would take us in the region on an hour to travel from Forteviot to the loch so it was an early night for us all and definitely no drink, for once. We also agreed that if we did get in amongst the geese would we drop some off for the gypsy families to enjoy.

This was another new area for us to explore, prior to this we had never heard of Loch Leven. There was an air of excitement about shooting on different land and because of the number of birds we had seen that afternoon we felt very positive.

We arrived on the field far too early the next morning, it was fairly easy to find and it didn't take long to put up the two hides and set out the decoys. Time then for a chill and enjoy a hot cup of coffee before getting all the shooting gear on.

We could hear geese calling from the loch; it was just starting to break light and there was restlessness amongst them as they were getting ready to take flight for their morning feed. We hadn't a clue what would happen but after seeing what had been in the area the day before it should be fairly easy to draw a few birds into us. It was strange not knowing exactly where we were and from which direction the geese would come. Obviously they would come from the loch behind us but when and how, we had no idea.

The first geese we saw were flying off in a totally different direction, towards the distant high ground and seemed to be landing on a field somewhere towards the top, just out of our sight. The loch erupted with the sounds of flying, gaggling, excited Pink-feet. Skein after skein of geese following the same flight path. We had seen thousands of geese before on our other land near Forteviot but what we were about to witness would surpass anything we had ever seen before.

As far as we could see all round us, there were geese. It didn't matter which way we looked there they were and it wasn't long before they began coming into our decoys. They weren't high and flew across the field, turned to make their final approach and came right in to us, at the most thirty yards away. Eight shots rattled off and six geese were lying dead on the field. We couldn't even move to pick them up as more geese were coming our way. It was a fast re-load and more geese succumbed to our shots. Our shooting that morning wasn't brilliant because many birds were missed. Maybe it was because they were too close or maybe it was just the sheer excitement once again as the adrenalin flowed. We shot four geese each in total and then as usual we left the field and let the geese come back in to land and continue feeding. Twenty geese were enough for any morning flight for five guns but we could have shot many more they were still coming into the field as we were gathering everything up. They didn't seem concerned about us in any way what-so-ever and that's something I had never seen before. Once off the field we drove to where the gypsies were staying and dropped off six geese for them. They asked us to stay and have a drink with them but we decided to make our way back to Forteviot but told them we would be back in the morning.

We sat in the car watching hundreds of geese going into a field on the higher ground. It was the same place we had seen them earlier that morning and even after two hours of daylight they were still coming off the loch and piling into the field. As far as we could see, there were geese heading towards that field, skein after skein after skein all shouting their heads off. After a quick check to make sure the field was still on the farmer's land we decided to go for a closer look; it was an opportunity not to be missed. The closest we could get to them was about a mile away but after watching skeins of geese still piling in we decided to try our luck and stalk them. We couldn't see the field the birds were dropping into but it appeared to be on the top boundary field. It would mean a very long walk and quite difficult terrain with gullies etc. but at least it was all uphill and the chance of the geese seeing us would be greatly reduced.

I wasn't too sure if I should go on this stalk as I had started sniffling and coughing quite a bit; I was starting with the symptoms of a cold or flu. After a bit of deliberation I felt I simply couldn't miss out but I would try desperately not to spook the geese with coughing; should we get close enough?

I won't bore you with all the details but cut more to the chase. It took towards an hour to reach the last field and get within range of the geese. It wasn't easy at all and still slightly uphill and by this time I was feeling completely knackered and sweating cobs with the symptoms of flu, 'man flu of course', After a breather it was going to be our final push and even when we were out in the wide open space of the stubble field the geese still poured in, ignoring us completely.

As we were resting we could see way down in the distance a police car had stopped and the policeman was walking around and looking at my car. Blackie was still in the back and that concerned me a little as I didn't know what the policeman wanted. Blackie was very protective of the car and would have snarled or barked at him. But it was certainly not going to get us fired up enough to go back to see what he wanted although it was a little concerning but this stalk had taken so long we weren't about to give up now. We watched him get back into his police car (through the binoculars) and he just sat there. Was he calling for back up or was he going to wait for our return, we simply didn't know, so we pushed on a bit further.

We were now only about thirty yards away from a small tight blackthorn hedgerow, the boundary of the field, after that it levelled out, perfectly flat. If we could manage to get to it and keep low we may be able to get shots at the geese. The old hedge itself wasn't very high and had quite a few large gaps in it so we got down and began a slow crawl which seemed to take forever. The noise coming from the field was now overwhelming. I was struggling holding back a cough as it would have given us away and if that had happened I would have been in deep poop with the others after such a long stalk.

We were in place tucked in behind the hedge and I raised my head a little to see where the geese were when a cock pheasant raised its head right in front of me. I froze, I didn't blink or breathe as it looked at me, if I had moved at all it would have given the game away and spooked the geese. For what seemed like an eternity but was probably just a few seconds the pheasant just kept on walking through the hedge, ignoring me completely. Geese were sat in front of us about twenty feet away, they were spread out all over the field in their thousands; it was blue with them gabbling away at each other. Some were fratching and falling out with each other but most of them were obliviously feeding on the stubble. They hadn't a clue we were there so we gingerly made ready to spring our ambush.

It was on the count of three when we stood up, there was silence for a split second before a tremendous roar as the geese took flight and became airborne. I tried to pick a bird but it was totally impossible and as I fired my first shot I could see the line of shot go straight through the mass of birds. Shots were going off rapidly and geese were dropping like flies. Eight shots had brought down twenty three geese. It was manic and the noise was ear splitting as the geese franticly flew back towards the loch.

We sat there in total disbelief we had pulled off something we had never thought possible. The stalk itself had been executed well; in every detail. "How the hell are we going to get all those geese back to the car", I asked? There was only one way I strapped seven geese to my dog lead and strung it around my shoulder but I still struggled to carry them. They soon became excruciatingly heavy, the dog lead was cutting into my shoulder and rubbing like hell and don't forget I was suffering with 'man flu'.

When we eventually got back to the car the policeman was still sat waiting for us and as we crossed the small road carrying our guns (in slips of course) and geese, we wondered if we were in some kind of trouble. As it turned out he was a really nice guy and was just concerned about my dog being left alone in the car. We chatted for a while and he promised he would keep an eye on our car if we ever went back. He was a keen shooting man himself and very involved in a local Pheasant syndicate. It was good to chat to a likeminded person and we were happy to give him a present of four geese; he left with a big smile on his face.

It was only day one and we had already shot forty three Pinkfeet and given away ten of them. We were left

A Wild Goose Chase

wondering how we were going to get them all back home. It was a good thing we were in two cars or we would have had to stop shooting and that wouldn't have gone down well at all. Yes, it was a large bag but every goose was eaten. I know I've said it before but I will not shoot more than I need and to this day it still applies, unless I'm shooting vermin, that is.

We had no need to do anymore goose shooting as we had enough geese to share between us all so we went fishing on the river Earn for two days and caught quite a few Sea Trout and also a fresh run Salmon weighing around nine pounds. A brilliant end to our few days away.

The Solway Marsh

For many years every late October or early November we would get the phone call we had all been waiting for. "The Geese are in on the Solway"

The Solway Marsh

As it was only about fifty miles away it was a great opportunity to enjoy some of the finest wild fowling available at that time.

A Wild Goose Chase

Every Sunday throughout the season we would go onto the Solway Marsh via Gretna Green. It was nearly always the same gang of dedicated goose shooters who went but sometimes others were invited depending on who could or couldn't go that morning. (We shared the costs of fuel.) As it only took us about an hour to get there it was simple and easy to arrange and we would normally leave Kendal around five to five thirty a.m. depending on who wanted picking up and from where.

Between us we had purchased a small, nine foot, solid wooden boat which would sit upside down perfectly on the roof rack of the car. That boat would get four of us across the river and onto the Rockcliffe Marsh. If there were ever more than four people which did happen occasionally, it would mean two trips across the river. This only happened though if we knew the tide was going to be out; it simply wasn't worth the risk.

It was a weekly Sunday morning ritual we would get out onto the marsh, shoot a few geese and be home before Sunday lunch time. There was always time to stop on our way home for a full English breakfast at a local truck stop. The afternoon could be then be spent with family or simply crashing out on the sofa.

Over the years I've had some amazing flights on both geese and Widgeon but as all fowlers know only too well on such a big salt marsh you can be sitting a mere fifty yards away, in the wrong place, then you just sit and watch them fly past. That happened more times to us than actually getting under the flight line of the geese. There were many, many blank mornings but it's the excitement of being there and watching those geese and hearing that magical sound of wink, wink from the Pink-foot. If you told someone who knew nothing about goose shooting and told them what time you got up and what you did to get near the geese, freezing or getting soaked to the skin, or covered in mud for absolutely nothing they would probably look at you as if you had lost the plot completely.

I could have written a full book all about the Solway expeditions but decided to write only about some of the more memorable trips. There were so many and when you think that we were on those marshes every Sunday for three and a half months every year, for many years, well that's a good many trips.

We got to know those marshes like the backs of our hands but still had to be extremely careful. We never took risks or did anything that would endanger any one of us. Things like knowing the tides and the sizes of the tides, wind conditions and also the gutters that would fill and cut you off completely if the larger tides came in while you were out on the marsh shooting. We never took any chances but over the years we've had a few things that scared the hell out of us. Unexpected things like the sand underfoot suddenly turning into quicksand and having to make a quick exit to safety; now that's very scary. Experience is a marvellous thing. After once getting lost in the fog and not being able to see a thing in front we always carried a compass; it saved us many times and led us safely back to land. It's one of the most eerie feelings when the fog comes in and you haven't a clue where you are because any previous landmarks are no longer visible. We call it the 'sound of silence', so it's always wise to have a compass because things can change in an instant on a marsh.

One particular morning we began our normal trip up the M6 and passing through Gretna Green and snaking our way down to the farm which was situated very close to the edge of the river overlooking the marsh. It was only a short distance to carry the boat and launch it, the ease of which depended on the tides and the height etc. At this point we were actually in Scotland but once across that river we were back in England. As long as we kept to the sands on the far side of the river we could shoot because shooting was not allowed on Sundays in Scotland. Some mornings a few lads would come across from Newcastle to shoot and a few of the locals we got to know over the years would also meet up with us and tell us what had been happening on the marsh during that week. At that time goose shooting wasn't as popular as it is now and I don't think the Solway has anywhere near the amount of geese it used to have; I doubt it ever could.

Once we had parked and somehow managed to slither out of the car, we removed the boat from the roof rack and changed into our fowling gear it was nice to sit, have a brew and check everything was ready before setting off. There is nothing worse than walking for an hour and then remembering you had left your shells or something else you needed in the car. Should that happen then it was tough because we wouldn't be going back until after the flight had finished. That was one of our rules.

This particular morning the tide was running fast, it was fairly close to high tide and we would have to row against an incoming current. It meant a long journey to get across to the sand on the opposite sea bank edge. We must have looked like Captain Pugwash and his crew with the four of us in a nine foot boat paddling like hell to get across as quickly as possible.

Once across, the boat was securely anchored; it would be a long, long walk up the marsh edge to get to where we would tuck in and hopefully get some shots at the geese. There were always gutters to navigate but this morning because of the tide the gutters were full so it took much longer to trace them further inland to find a safer place to jump or wade across.

The wind was blowing strongly from the south west which would mean the geese would be flying straight into it to get inland to feed. It could take us anywhere from thirty minutes to fifty minutes to get into our much used foxholes. These had been dug into the mash by others over the years because it was a very popular flight line. We always tried our very best to get there first before anyone else jumped in and claimed them. Some of the gutters were treacherous and very large to cross and over the years quite a number of guns finished up with wet, frozen feet after slipping back down them and sea water going over the tops of their waders. I had it happen to me a few times and in January it's not at all pleasant.

As we walked towards the foxholes and at the first sign of it breaking light it was normal for the Widgeon to start moving inland. They would be making their way back out onto the Solway estuary to roost after feeding all night. They would be in their thousands whistling away with that distinctive Widgeon whistle, flying at the most about forty yards up. They were and have been the most widgeon I have ever seen in one mass. I'm certainly not exaggerating; one cloud of them would be over two hundred yards in length. I couldn't imagine the amount of Widgeon in that one mass and there were more than three masses of Widgeon like that each morning. Somehow, they always seemed to beat us, I would have loved to have been sat in the gutter with my Zabala ten bore side by side in my hands loaded with two and a quarter

A Wild Goose Chase

ounces of number fours, three and a half inch magnums as they flew over. How could you miss?

It was always a long walk up to the shooting grounds and there was always lots of banter, especially for any new goose shooters joining us. I have learned over the years, when walking to always have my jacket open and unzipped to prevent overheating and sweating even in January when it's a minus figure. When you sweat heavily and then stop walking it is possible to become extremely cold and freeze, it can then be a struggle to warm back up; again this comes with experience.

Although I have many enjoyable memories of shooting on the Solway this particular memory always comes to mind whenever I think or talk about the marsh.

I was lying behind a ridge of muddy sand in a very deep gutter and looking at the distant hills recognising the familiar landmarks when I saw a dark cloud moving from right to left. It seemed very strange, although it was a few miles away it appeared to be moving very quickly. It hadn't occurred to me that it was geese on the move but they weren't flying like Pinks or even Greylags. They started to turn and head towards the marsh and they were coming straight towards us but still a few miles away. As they got closer the black cloud was getting bigger, it was then we heard a faint noise coming from them.

A Wild Goose Chase

What a strange noise it was, it was like hundreds of terriers yapping in unison but it was coming from the geese and every bird was doing the same call; yap; yap; yap. They came closer and closer, the noise increased to a deafening pitch somewhat like a train going passed at full speed. Within a few minutes they were flying over us; they were the famous Barnacle geese. Barnacle geese always wintered on the Solway coast and it was an incredible sight to witness.

Barnacle Goose

There were thousands upon thousands of geese in one almighty mass milling around the marsh and looking for a place to pitch in; flying over us at only about twenty feet up. I once had about twenty birds land within ten feet of my gutter. It was a sight and sound once again, never to be forgotten and over the years I've witnessed them coming onto the Rockcliffe marsh many, many times. The Barnacle

Goose is a protected species of goose and that flight was possibly one of the most incredible sights ever to be witnessed. Most of them came from a nearby bird sanctuary called Calaverock but they loved feeding on Rockcliffe marsh.

It was now breaking light quite quickly and the temperature was dropping fast. The sound from the Pinks, sat out on the estuary, was getting noisier as they were becoming more restless and getting ready to become airborne to fly inland once again to their nearby feeding grounds. That was the most exciting time of the morning because you may just get a few early skeins coming over quite low and this offered a greater chance of getting a few shots at them.

We had a strong south westerly wind that particular morning so maybe our chances were a little bit better as it might just keep the birds down a little. A few shots were echoing from the other side of the marsh, this meant either the ducks or geese were now starting to move.

Suddenly there was a deathly silence out on the estuary; this is normal just before the geese start to lift. I was right and within minutes there was that long awaited and pleasing sound of geese calling and coming towards us. As we looked from the marsh, where we were hidden, towards the Solway estuary itself, line after line of geese were now heading towards us.

A small skein of about fifteen birds was heading my way and as soon as they were just out in front of me I stood up and picked a bird. I let the first shot go from my ten bore and then swung onto another bird as the skein went directly over my head. Blackie had run into shot as he always did and was now chasing across the marsh, behind me, at full speed. I lost him completely for a few minutes but he came plodding back with a Pink-foot firmly in his mouth. Most of the other lads were getting a few shots but I couldn't see if they were getting hits or not.

Everywhere you looked geese were in the air and heading towards us. Some would be wide of us and some too high but it was normal to see the air towards the estuary stacked full of flying geese. My next shot hit one smack in the front and it turned back towards the sands obviously hit very hard. Blackie was right on it and continued to chase it as it glided back towards the safety of the sands. I lost sight of him altogether; he was just like a dot on the landscape. As he continued and followed it across the sands he put up another thousand geese or more that were still roosting; I then lost sight of him altogether. Fortunately he came back as pleased as punch with a Pink-foot in his mouth but then looked at me as if to say; hit them harder next time please. Sorry Blackie but it was one hell of a retrieve, yet again.

The flight off the estuary always seemed to start just after eight o'clock and we used to be able to set our clocks for when the flight was going to start. It could go on for at least an hour and then it would be the long walk back to the boat, row back across the river and a short walk to the car; hopefully carrying a few geese. Many a time though we would return with very little but it was the magic of being out there on the Solway, hearing and witnessing that amazing sight?

One of the things we always looked forward to was calling at the truck stop for breakfast on our way home, by then we were ready for it. Over the years we got to know the staff very well and one of the ladies who nearly always served us used to say. "Here are my boys, four full English breakfasts on the way and four cups of builder's tea". That tea was so strong you could have stood a spoon up in it but it went down lovely.

At the end of every season we would take her a big box of chocolates as a thank you with a little card saying, see you next year and thanks once again. We always signed it, The Goose Shooting Boys from Kendal.

The Solway Moon Flight

Over the years I have shot quite a few moon flights on the Solway and this night was just one of them. It was always better if there was large evening tide around eleven o'clock or towards midnight as there was a chance this would shift a few geese onto and into the marsh which would increase our chances considerably.

We always parked at a hotel called the Metal Bridge Hotel and would normally get there after it was closed and everyone had gone home. Next to the hotel was a river, the same river we had to row across at Gretna. We would follow it until we came to the marsh itself and then head inwards towards the centre looking for some deepish gutters or cuts to sit in and conceal ourselves for a while.

I always had my dog Blackie with me and he just loved being out on the marsh. To be out there without a dog would have made it very difficult to pick up any shot or wounded geese. The thing about Blackie is he would always run into shot and sometimes return with a bird I thought I had missed; it happened on many an occasion. Without him I wouldn't have had a clue if I had hit one, pulling it out as some shots were taken so quickly and you were soon onto the second shot. He wasn't the best trained dog and made lots of mistakes but to me he was brilliant and just loved the goose shooting. As I told you earlier, he suffered with goose fever just like me. What a pair we were. (Smiles)

It was a still night with a slight frost and the occasional bang could be heard from other guns in the distance that were having a shot at ducks or geese. There certainly were a lot of geese moving around the marsh that evening so we moved and walked further in to an area where we thought they would be.

Every so often a single BOOOOOOOM came from what sounded like a single four bore, the noise was so loud it would scatter the geese in every direction and they would franticly look for somewhere else to land safely. BOOOOOOOOM off it went again. Ten minutes later BOOOOOOOOM off it went again, it was then we heard someone shout loudly from across the river. "Will you stick that blasted gun up your arse" All went quiet after that and we had a bit of a chuckle; Mr four bore must have upset other shooters who were also out after the geese.

There was a little bit of cloud cover so it was possible to silhouette the geese and get shots but getting closer to them

A Wild Goose Chase

was getting very frustrating as we would be spotted fairly easy on the dead flat, salt marsh. When this happened the birds would move off somewhere else, well out of range; this happened often. It was certainly a wild goose chase that evening. Steph was going to go for a walk around the marsh and I was going to stay put, the idea was for him to try and push a few geese towards me. It made a lot of sense really, splitting up and we arranged to meet back up in an hours' time.

I was starting to feel the cold now and ice was forming on my moustache and wished I could have changed places with Steph, walking rather than just sitting still; at least I would have been warmer. I tried distracting myself by watching some of the distant geese, which were plentiful and still flying around the marsh.

After about thirty minutes two shots went off about a mile away and I could hear geese coming my way; was it Steph getting in amongst them? It was difficult holding Blackie down in the shallow gutter as he had also heard the geese and wanted to be up and at them. He was a pain in the arse sometimes with his habit of running into shot.

It was then that I heard the distinctive call of a few Pinks just out in front of me, so got myself poised and ready to take a shot, should I get the chance. They sounded very close and within seconds they were on me. Up went the gun and two quick shots hit their targets perfectly and seconds later I heard two thumps on the ground behind me. I had just taken a very fast left and right on two Pinks; yeah....... Perfect, brilliant shooting even if I say so myself. Blackie had already gone to pick them and I sat waiting patiently for him to return with my prize. He came into vision and to my horror he was carrying a dead Barnacle Goose. 'Oh My God', I had just shot two protected geese. Blackie returned with the second one and I remember thinking, what the hell do I do now? I stuffed them into the inside pocket of my Parker poaching pocket, panicking and went back to where I had arranged to meet Steph. I hid them in the gutter just in case anyone came near and could see what I had just done.

I had about a thirty minute wait before Steph returned and the first words he asked me were. "What's all that white fluff in your hair"? Whilst waiting I had decided to pluck the geese and get rid of the evidence. I managed to get the head, wings and feet off using a small pocket knife, it was now time for a very fast exit off the marsh after burying the remains. Oh, and I must tell you, they were possibly the nicest geese I've ever tasted.

I told myself that I would never shoot Barnacle geese again and I never did. I was gutted when it happened but I was not about to waste lives taken by a stupid and silly mistake; it was a lesson learned.

A Wild Goose Chase

Don't Shoot the Spies

Once again, it was another organised pilgrimage to Scotland but this time it was going to be with Cam, Dave and my brother-in- law Chris. Mid November and we were going with Cam in his father's new Range Rover. Range Rovers hadn't been out very long and it was sheer luxury travelling in such an amazing 4x4. Sat up in the air and being able to see over walls and hedgerows was fantastic. We felt like 'Lords of the Manor'; the idle rich; well, we can all dream.

We could have gone to Loch Leven or Forteviot or even Methven but it was suggested we went to the Crief area again. We had been before but thought we could maybe find some new farms to shoot on. Goose shooters tend not to say exactly where they have been as they are always very protective of the land they have and don't want it ruined by idiots! If I was ever asked where I shot the geese my reply for years was always the same; Scotland.

We set off early Sunday morning and the plan was to get there fairly early, look around for feeding geese and then hopefully get permission to have a go at them. I did know of one particular farm where we could go in the Crief area and if all else failed we could ask for permission to shoot there. I really did want to have a go at the Greylags as I hadn't shot many before.

We came into Crief the most direct way, rather than via Perth and Methven and arrived about lunch time so we had lots of time to have a good nosey about. As we travelled through Crief we could see a number of Greylags flying towards a farm a few miles ahead of us. After a closer look there certainly were plenty of them and they were dropping in just behind the back of quite a large farm. It was difficult to see exactly where, as it would mean going up a very long concrete drive to the farm first then going behind it to locate them to get a much better view.

Of course it was my turn to ask the farmer as no one else seemed up for it; it was regularly my turn so I suppose the others thought I had the 'gift of the gab'. As we pulled into the farm yard we saw three men dipping sheep in a mobile dipping machine. It stunk of medicated dip and they looked rather busy as there were a great number of sheep penned up. It maybe wasn't the right time to be asking but nothing ventured, nothing gained. The three of them stood staring at us; the atmosphere appeared to be a little hostile, no-one smiled or even acknowledged us.

A Wild Goose Chase

I stepped out of the Range Rover feeling rather apprehensive and walked towards the three chaps who were dipping the sheep. After asking to speak to the owner this guy came right up to me and said. "That's me, what do you want"? He was very abrupt and his manner quite aggressive. By this time my backside was twitching and I waffled on a about being on holiday from England and that we were looking for some goose shooting. I told him we had been watching the geese dropping into his fields and wondered if he would allow us on his land.

He came straight towards me, grabbed me by the scruff of my collar and said. "If ya gonna shoot the geese ya will shoot them the noo." "I can't", I replied it's Sunday and shooting isn't allowed in Scotland on a Sunday. He stared at me and said in another loud voice. "If you don't shoot them the noo, you can leave right now, I'm sick of them blasted birds."

Phew it was one hell of an introduction and I was getting more anxious by the second, he had reacted somewhat violently towards me and was very scary. He took me to one side, out of earshot of the other two farm workers and I explained yet again that it was against the law to shoot on a Sunday in Scotland. If the Police saw us doing such a thing we would be in deep shit, possibly jailed and our guns taken from us. We would also lose our shotgun certificates and probably never get them back. He started to calm down a little; he'd probably had a crap day dipping the sheep and asked where we were staying. When I had told him it was The Methven Arms Hotel his eyes lit up and he said, "I will meet you there later tonight and we will discuss the matter further."

I shook his hand and thanked him profusely although I was extremely baffled by the change in his attitude. I turned around to walk back to the car and saw that Cam had turned it around completely with my car door wide open ready to get the hell out of it. They were bricking it; they'd seen the farmer's reaction towards me and thought we were getting thrown off the farm. I assured them that all was okay and had arranged to meet the farmer later in the hotel.

Within a mile of that farm was another farm where we had actually never shot but had permission to go back at any time. We dropped by to say hello to the farmer as we made our way back to the hotel; he also had a few hundred Greylag geese feeding on a large potato field.

Things were looking up even if we didn't get the shooting on the previous farm. At least now we would get a chance to get in amongst them on this farm; the farmer was only too happy for us to get rid of a few geese. We continued our way back to Methven and checked into the hotel feeling quite optimistic about the shooting for the next few days.

About five o'clock and after having a bit of a siesta we sorted the shooting gear and nipped down for our evening meal; meals were included in our stay and of course they were amazing and great value for money. Oh and before I forget they allowed Blackie into our bedroom to sleep so I suppose it was a bit of luxury for him also. He was used to being indoors at home and once on his rug he would never move until asked.

I knew the owners of the hotel fairly well as I had stopped there a few times before; I was also fairly well acquainted with some of the locals. One in particular whose name was The Bandit; so called because he had lost his arm in the war, many years earlier. Bandit lived in a prefab just outside the village, paid for by the Scottish government. His face looked as if a Land Rover had run over it and then reversed back over it a few times; talk about craggy features. He was such a good laugh and kept tormenting me to play him at pool for a little wager. Why would I want to rob a one armed pool player I asked? I was actually quite good at Pool. Well! When I did play him for a small wager, he totally hammered me and then just winked at me after taking my money and a wee dram, the bugger. I also found out later that he made some amazing hand carved bird tables; not bad really, for a one armed guy. I just wish I had a picture of them for you to see, the detail in the carving, using only one hand was amazing.

That evening the drinks were flowing, we had deep pockets and holes in our glasses; the holiday mood had certainly kicked in. At one stage Cam asked us if we wanted a bag of nuts and after visiting the bar he came back with a card full of them, he had bought the lot. Ah, well, the influence of drink, it makes us do all sorts of weird and wonderful things! At another stage there must have been twelve of us stood at the bar, going down the line round after round. I remember one of the locals asking, when it was his round if I wanted a wee half to which I replied, "I'd prefer a pint please." I wasn't to know it meant a wee half of whisky. Boy was I embarrassed and the locals had a bit of a giggle about it, bloody English, he muttered. Fortunately, I hadn't drunk much when the farmer we met earlier in the day came in to see us. Two of us bought him a drink and sat down with him. What a difference in his attitude and he apologised for being a bit rude earlier but his day hadn't gone at all to plan and I had got the brunt of it.

By way of an apology he had arranged for us to meet his keeper at six o'clock the next morning on a small lane that ran behind the back of his farm. His keeper would take us out on the geese for the morning flight because he wanted them shifting off his fields. We had no idea he had a keeper and he explained to us about the Pheasant shooting syndicate he and a few of the locals were involved in. I asked him why his keeper hadn't shifted the geese for him and he told me he was far too busy as they reared and released over ten thousand Pheasants. Hence the keeper coming out with us in the morning, probably to keep an eye on us and make sure we didn't bother his Pheasants. It came as a bit of a shock because he didn't look like a shooting man at all but then who does I suppose is the question? Apparently, he owned acres and acres of land and large amounts of woodland so I assumed he was a fairly wealthy man and he was certainly dressed accordingly.

After far too many drinks it was bed time and that's the last I remember of that evening until the alarm clock hammered in my ear the next morning at five o'clock. Cam and Dave were up and getting ready and came into our bedroom for a coffee. It was then suggested that we split up into two teams. Dave and Cam would go onto the potato field and Chris and I would go and meet the keeper. They would come and pick us up after the flight had finished. Cam took us to where we had to meet the keeper who was sat in his little white van waiting patiently for us. A quick unload of the Range Rover and Cam and Dave headed off to the other farm. This large stocky guy came out of the van followed by one of the fattest and widest Labs I had ever seen, it was obviously getting on a bit in years as it wobbled and struggled, following closely behind him.(Bless it)

After a hand shake and introductions it became very noticeable that the guy had a very different accent and quite a severe speech impediment. He had been a Polish prisoner of war and had a slight Scottish accent mixed in with Polish; he also stuttered severely. I know it was wrong for us to look at each other and smile but it was rather difficult to understand a single word he said. We were told to leave our hides and decoys behind the nearby hedgerow because he had already set out a hide for us and he had also placed out forty silhouette decoys ready on the field. He had rolled two of the large straw bales together and used sacking to camouflage both front and back so we could get inside.

As we were feeling very delicate from the previous night we simply tagged on behind and followed him uphill over a couple of fields, not saying much to each other at all. The hide suddenly appeared in front of us and we got inside, all three of us plus two dogs. I was worried in case the dogs decided to have a go at each other because it was so cramped inside that small hide. All I could smell on Chris's breath was the stale smell of whisky from the night before and he looked as if he was still a little drunk. How could I tell? Well, his eyes were like pee holes in the snow, just two little slits trying their best to focus. Whilst we were waiting we had another very large coffee from the flask, a bit of a chat with the keeper, trying not to let Chris's breath get in his face. It would have knocked him over and out of the hide.

A Wild Goose Chase

The morning after the night before

It was starting to break light and we were looking forward to getting a few Greylags in the bag when two birds seemed to appear from nowhere flying at about ten foot high across the field in front of us. Chris grabbed his gun, I was also ready and we peered through a tiny gap in the sacking to see where they were. As they got closer Chris stood up to shoot and the keeper pushed him back down very sharply, saying "Ya, Ya Dunna, Dunna, Dunna Sh..Sh.. Sh.. Shoot the Sp..Sp..Spies." Well we were shocked to say the least; we had just missed a perfect chance of bagging two Pink-footed geese. I looked at Chris and he was staring back at me in total disbelief, still not sober but getting better by the minute after the bollocking. We hadn't to shoot the spies? What blooming spies? We thought we would be shooting Greylags because the previous

A Wild Goose Chase

day we had seen Greylags dropping into that very same field but it was two Pinks that had come in at first light.

They flew around the field a few more times and seemed to cover every angle possible as they flew low over every bit of that field but never once attempted to land. So was this guy right or not? We weren't too sure about him at all. For about five minutes they flew around that field like Springer Spaniels quartering every bit of it and we could have shot them at least three or four times but NO!!!. WE MUST NOT SHOOT THE SPIES. Then, they just flew away over the bottom left corner of the field straight over a distant gateway. It was then that the keeper told us that they would come back later, in greater numbers and they would come in right over that gateway. Yeah, right we thought. The spies had done their job, what a load of cobblers.

Quite a few shots were coming from Cam and Dave from the other farm and it was obvious that they were having much more fun than we were. Another ten minutes passed and nothing, another ten minutes and nothing. The sun was just starting to come through over the horizon, between the distant hills and the low mist of the morning giving it a hazy shimmer. More shots came from the other lads and we were now getting a bit peed off to say the least.

The sun was now shining brightly and we hadn't heard a single goose or seen any signs of them, it was then the keeper

A Wild Goose Chase

said he would have to leave and go to feed his Pheasants. My first thought was, "oh, no… is that it for us now"? He suggested we stay in the hide a bit longer and promised us the birds would come back for definite but not to stop too late, if we could possibly avoid it.

We sat bored to tears and it didn't help much hearing more shots coming from the other two lads. At least they were getting a shot or two, that's far more than what we were getting. We even began hoping that they were missing everything; not very sporting of us, I know.

It was now towards nine o'clock and we were wondering if we should pack up and walk back down to the lane to meet Cam and Dave. By the sounds of it and the lack of shots their flight was over and ours hadn't even begun. We had until ten o'clock to get back to the hotel and get our breakfast; my stomach was starting to rumble just thinking about it and it was just settling from the previous night's intake of alcohol.

Well, that was it; we put the guns into their slips and started walking back when we heard the sound of geese calling. We looked behind us and could see them in the distance behind the gateway. It was the same gateway the spies had flown over earlier that morning and they looked as if they were coming towards us. We ran back and got the guns ready as quickly as we could. Blackie was pulled into the hide with us

A Wild Goose Chase

because he could hear them and wanted to get a better look by sitting outside the hide. Guess what? They came right over that very gateway, probably a few hundred of them and they were shouting very loudly and spiralling down from quite a height.

They looked as if they were going to come straight into the decoys but then at the last minute they went for another lap of the field and then turned back towards us again. As they came closer to the decoys Chris said "let them land, let them land" so we kept our heads down as low as we possibly could. Within seconds they were all in and it had gone extremely quiet, the geese were probably wondering what the silhouette decoys were. We got up together and spooked them into flying and after four fast successive shots; six geese were lying on the ground, stone dead. We had done it perfectly; it couldn't have been executed any better.

We just couldn't believe what the keeper had said to us earlier but it did happen, exactly as he said it would. So were they spies or not? I'm sure they were because the geese did come back after the spies had done their check of the field and then came back later, flying over the exact same area. It was exactly what he said would happen; or was it more good luck?

There are always lessons to learn and that morning we did learn something new and we saw it happen quite a few times over the years that followed but this time we knew what to look out for.

Cam and Dave had also been amongst a few geese and shot five Greylags. Our total for the morning was five Greylags and six Pinks and that was only our first morning.

Chris with the Pinks

During our next two days shooting we returned to the potato field and bagged another fourteen Greylags. A very reputable bag of twenty five birds and just perfect for the back of the Range Rover.

We never went back to that farm in all the years that we revisited Scotland and I often thought about the Polish keeper. It wasn't that we didn't want to shoot there again; it was just that we had so many farms available to us in that area. Those were the days. Within a few years we had broadened our horizons and found other areas to shoot, we travelled all over but mainly northwards chasing the geese. Places like the Orkneys, Montrose Basin, Blairgowrie, Pitlochry, Couper Angus, Fife, Isle of Skye, Bute, just to name a few but there were many other amazing places. Every area we visited had magnificent scenery and we always met some very interesting characters.

Over the years goose shooting became more popular and many southerners were travelling north and obviously getting some good shooting. We were very lucky to have so many contacts and areas we could go to but as the years passed, things changed, as they do. People began cashing in and making lots of money out of goose shooting, gone were the days when you could shoot for a bottle or two of whisky, or even the farmer paying to have the birds moved off his fields. Oh well, at least I was fortunate enough to be involved before it all changed.

Widgeon on the Solway

Every Sunday during the winter months would be spent on the Solway Marsh, mainly morning flighting. As I mentioned before, although it was in Gretna Green in Scotland, we had to row across the river to be back in England where it was perfectly legal to shoot wildfowl on a Sunday.

On this particular morning there were four of us and as usual we arrived in plenty of time, so it was a coffee and a chill before the long walk up the marsh to get to our favourite shooting grounds. It was always the same ritual and most of the time we would take the 'micky' out of each other in some way or another. The banter always flowed and if we had anyone new (a rookie goose shooter) with us they would get it full on. Looking back, some of the stories we used to tell the rookies were, hmmm, not always truthful and a number of times we would wind them up and confuse them so much they really didn't know what to expect; but it was all good clean fun.

It was a severe frost that morning in the middle of January and a fairly strong northerly wind was cutting right through our clothing. This created around a minus ten centigrade wind chill factor. It was certainly a Damart thermal morning with plenty of layers to keep us warm. Everything from thermal socks, waders, an extra jumper, heavy insulated jacket, neck ties, warm gloves, warmer trousers and not forgetting the most important piece of equipment, the Thermos flask and maybe even a bacon butty. My Zabala 10 bore side by side was in its slip and I always took a long thumb stick to check areas for depths of water in the gutters, it was a must. We looked very much like the Michelin man, (a tyre advert from years ago), on manoeuvres.

That particular morning the tide was just on the ebb, so there was still a large area of water to row across, plus there was quite a strong current to navigate. All four of us would have to paddle and get across as fast as we could to prevent the current taking us too far down the river. It also meant that when we returned to the boat it would have to be carried quite a distance to get back to the river as the tide would have receded greatly.

Once on the other side we noticed a further two boats were already anchored. One was Danny's (a local lad) and the other belonged to the lads from Newcastle. Seeing Danny's transport would have left you wondering how the hell he ever got across the river. It resembled an old metal bath tub, just big enough for one person and a paddle that had once been a broom handle, it had a square of plywood nailed onto the end to make the paddle. Painted on it were the words, MOON SOOSE. We think it should have said 'Moon Goose' but he wasn't the brightest 'button in the box' and we gave him the benefit of the doubt maybe the paint had run a little bit before drying, anyway it always gave us a good laugh when we saw it. If I had to describe Danny I would have said that he was quite small and had a very well lived in, craggy, looking face. He had an obsession with goose shooting and he would be across on the marsh whenever he could. He was also a great source of knowledge with regards to the info on the geese such as where they were or a least where they were likely to be flighting. We had become great pals over the years so we decided to go and find him and get him to bring us up to speed. We knew roughly which gutter he would be laying in, he, like us all had his favourite places on the marsh and we could guarantee he'd be in one of them. So finding him would be relatively easy.

We were only about a third of the way up the marsh and had to go inland much further because of the amount of water still lying in the gutters as the tide was still receding. We had plenty of time to get where we were going but the reason we were out much earlier that morning was to try and intercept the Widgeon for once. This was something we had never attempted before because we knew it would be extremely difficult to get under them especially on such a large marsh. We did have a rough idea though where they would probably cross over it and we knew they would be returning to the safety of the Solway sands at the first glimpse of light.

We could hear the occasional sound of the Pinks shouting way out on the estuary and it was important for us to get into position long before they started lifting. The idea was to stop about two thirds of the way up the marsh and try our best to intercept the Widgeon before continuing to our usual positions and hopefully ambush the geese on their flight inland.

There was a sudden shout from one of the lads who had seen massive bunches of Widgeon now making their way towards us. Two of us were stuck in the middle of a very deep and wide gutter, trying our best to get across it as safely as possible. The other two had started to run further up the marsh to find somewhere to get well hidden in what little cover there was available. We did get across in time and were able to tuck ourselves under the ridge of a gutter totally out of view of the Widgeon. In the panic though, the water had gone over the tops of both our waders and our feet were now soaked and they were beginning to feel very cold indeed. I had managed to get out the ten bore and had it loaded, ready and waiting. Out of the corner of my eye I could see my friend about twenty yards to my right; he was also tucked under the edge of the gutter waiting in anticipation.

The Widgeon were coming towards us in their thousands and we could hear the very distinctive sound of Widgeon whistling. The memories and sounds are unforgettable no matter how long you live. A massive black cloud of them were flying back to the safety of the estuary; a few miles behind them were more, vast clouds, following the same flight line. It's at that time the adrenalin starts to kick in and you're doing your very best not to get too excited and jump up too soon.

I knew they were close and had a quick 'look-see' to see exactly where they were. They were going to go right over us and seemed to be low enough for once as they battled hard against the northerly wind. I stood up, it was impossible to take aim and select a bird and the noise was deafening. I aimed straight into the black mass of birds and pulled the front trigger. I got an almighty jolt in my shoulder, both barrels had discharged together; I hated it when my ten bore did that. It threw me hurtling backwards into the gutter, completely knocking me off my feet. My friend had not even fired a shot and as I picked myself up I shouted to him. "Why didn't you shoot?" it was then I saw his silhouette, he was on his knees, holding his head in both hands. I ran over to him and could see that he was bleeding from the corner of his eye and nose, he was in a bit of a state but more shocked than hurt. It was hard not to laugh, he had been hurt but even he could see the funny side as he told me what had happened. Apparently, as he stood up to shoot, one of my dead birds had travelled straight down his gun barrel and smacked him in his face and had also knocked his safety catch back. What a start to the morning, he was quite sore and had the beginnings of a black eye and I had a big bruise on my left shoulder from both barrels going off at the same time and soggy cold feet. We met up with the other two lads who had managed to shoot Widgeon and between us we totalled twelve. The noise of the first shots turned the other remaining birds and they veered off slightly out of our range; this meant no-one else on the marsh would get a shot at them. We left the dead birds in the gutter, well-hidden and would pick them up on our way back.

We decided to look for Danny before we pushed further up the marsh to lay in wait for the Pinks. We found him and he told us that for most of the week the numbers of geese on the marsh had increased greatly, Pinks, that is and he suggested we try one our favourite places, called the 'Pitts or Foxholes'. This was an area that had been dug out many years ago but once in the pit you were totally hidden and could only shoot geese that flew directly overhead; this of course was quite restrictive at times but when it worked it worked so well. Unfortunately the flight that morning wasn't very productive and only two Pinks were shot. Many of the geese flew off on a different flight line but it was still amazing to watch. It was normal for a flight to last about an hour but occasionally it was longer and then the skeins would sometimes fly lower offering us a better chance; but that morning it wasn't to be.

On the way back we picked up the Widgeon and were making our way back to the boat when one of the lads noticed a considerable amount of splashing coming from one of the flashes left behind by the tide. After closer inspection and to our complete and utter surprise a Conger Eel had managed to get its self-trapped in the flash, unable to return with the ebbing tide. This was an opportunity not to be missed but no one was willing to shoot. In fact we had enough to carry with the Widgeon and geese. It would have possibly died anyway as the water receded so I took out my ten bore. This time I only loaded one shell as I didn't want knocking off my feet again with two barrels going off at the same time. I shot at it and hit it at the back of the head; there was the most unbelievable thrashing of water you could ever imagine. The eel came up out of the water and onto the grass, slithering for a few seconds and then, that was it, it was dead; it never moved again. We must have jumped a few feet back when it happened; it completely took us by surprise. Then the realisation, how the hell do we get it back to the car? I shot it so I had to carry it. I took off my belt and fastened it around its head, then fastened my dog lead to the belt and dragged it back along the sands. It was about five foot long and weighed 'a ton' and at times I wished I had just left it where it was. I also wondered what I was going to do with it when I got home. The stink in the car whilst travelling home was indescribable so I decided to take the eel to my Dad who could cook it for his trail hounds. OMG, as long as I live I am never going near a Conger Eel again, and would never ever, attempt to eat one. The smell of it cooking was absolutely disgusting and it stayed in my nostrils for ages. The smell is impossible to describe, and trust me you don't want to know because it was so gross.

In all the years that followed and our numerous visits to the Solway we never went after the Widgeon again but to do it once and to have so many come over us in one enormous mass, well the experience was absolutely amazing. I doubt it will ever happen again and often wonder if shooters on the marsh today still have the same amount of Widgeon; I doubt it very much but you just never know.

Crief with a Goose Guide

Looking back at the number of times I shot in the Crief area and it certainly was a great number of times, one in particular stands out. It was also a stressful time but funny in many ways. Once again the holidays from the K Shoe factory were getting closer and it was that time of year again. Do we book a comfortable hotel or rough it again in places like 'Rats Paradise', for our annual goose pilgrimage to Scotland. It was usual to meet up in a local pub, have a few beers and decide where and what we were going to do for the three days goose shooting. Well, it was as good an excuse as any other and it kept the wives/girlfriends happy as they could come and have a catch up with friends.

This time four of us would be going and after a lot of deliberation it was agreed. Instead of Methven or some of the other places we could have gone we decided on a trip to the Crief area. One of the lads had seen an advert in a shooting magazine offering three full days of morning goose flights, an afternoon on pheasants and also a few evening goose and duck flights. I telephoned the guy and booked the required number of days, it sounded excellent value indeed. We certainly weren't being over charged and we would be staying with the guide in a massive log cabin in the woods near Crief. Included in the price were packed lunches and all our meals. For once everything would be taken care of and meant that there would be no travelling around, following skeins of geese and asking permission to shoot. This would make a nice change and we wouldn't be as tired or crabby after late nights and very early mornings; we could maybe get some rest in between the shooting.

As usual we travelled up early Sunday morning and arranged to meet the guide about lunch time. I remember pulling into the car park of a local hotel in Crief and getting out to meet him. He stepped out of his Ranger Rover, he was massive, a mountain of a man. He was dressed in a kilt complete with sporran, thick woolly socks including a dirk; the traditional Scottish outfit. He was built like a brick *hithouse and slowly walked towards us smiling from ear to ear, big red beard and all. To say he was a character is an understatement; he had us laughing within the first few minutes. He was certainly a very jovial character and had a larger than life personality who certainly put us at ease from the moment we met him. The only downside about him was he never shut up droning on and on about what he had done during his keepering days. He had massive calf muscles and it was apparent that he had done a lot walking and stalking; he was an expert on deer, as we were later to find out.

We enjoyed a few coffees and went through the itinerary for the three days goose shooting. It was clear to us after a brief chat that the estate where he worked had been suffering financially over the last few years with regard to the deer stalking bookings. His boss had suggested taking out shooting parties on the geese and ducks and have a few walked up Pheasant days to subsidise the estates income. We jumped into our vehicle and followed him to the log cabin that we would be staying. It was absolutely out of this world and situated on the high ground just off the edge of a forest with the most beautiful, outstanding views. We were introduced to his wife who was also very charming. She was a very attractive lady and had the personality to go with it. We had never before stayed in such a delightful setting and with people who simply couldn't do enough for us; this was going to be a very comfortable few days.

Once unpacked the guide said he would take us out and show us the field where we would be shooting the following morning. Although we knew the region quite well we were taken to a new area of land, completely unknown to us. It was situated in the Crief valley and was predominately stubble fields with the occasional turnip and potato field. It was a very warm early autumn Sunday afternoon and we were in short sleeves looking over the field when the guide shouted us over to look at something. He pointed to the ground at what looked like old worm casts in amongst the barley stubble and told us that was where the geese put their beaks at night when they were sleeping. "There must have been lots of them on here last night; he said, in a very excited voice, there are hundreds of them".

Well, I thought he was either joking or testing us and I quickly looked at the others but they were looking as confused as me also. He was being absolutely serious and he honestly believed he was right. He walked off looking for more, leaving us wondering what the hell was going on. Whispering to each other, "Is this guy for real"? OMG, what do we say to him now? Well, we decided to say nothing and let him continue talking. It quickly became apparent that he knew very little at all about goose shooting.

He asked us to stay where we were; he was going to the farm to bring his Range Rover across the stubble so we could have a drink of juice and a chat about where we would place the hides the next morning. All four of us were very bemused and stunned by what he had said and as far as we could make out there were no goose droppings, not even a feather on that field. One of us would have to say something and very soon.

A Wild Goose Chase

Everything was well arranged in the boot of the Range Rover, fold up seats, fruit, cold and hot drinks and a number of snacks. We couldn't fault his hospitality in any way but his knowledge of shooting geese seemed like zilch. One of the lads asked how long he had been taking groups out, he told us this was his second year. He'd had a terrific season last year and not one complaint. It was during our conversation that he came out with another statement which threw us, yet again. "We will come onto this field after breakfast, Okay"? Things were really starting to worry us now. We challenged him and he told us that we wouldn't see any geese until about ten o'clock so why come out so early. We told him we had been shooting the wild geese in that area for many years and had become quite knowledgeable and were very experienced in morning flights. We told him you needed to get up an hour before first light and get set up with the hides and decoys and then sit and wait. He had never heard of it before and couldn't understand it but reluctantly agreed to do it our way. Thank God for that, if he hadn't agreed we would most probably have left.

We hadn't had a shot and were already wondering whether to knock it on the head, leave and go somewhere else to shoot. That evening for dinner we were served soup, salmon and steaks with lots of fresh veggies and homemade sweets. The food was delicious and plenty of it. Dinner was followed by a few drams of a nice malt whisky which rounded off the evening very nicely. Well, we had paid a quite large deposit so there wouldn't be a massive bill to pay after the shooting. After the evening meal we had a chance to discuss the previous afternoon and it was agreed we would stay for the morning flight before deciding whether or not to stay with him or simply move on. If we did get amongst the geese then it would be a holiday to remember and a good story to re-tell.

With the weather being very warm for the time of year we dressed accordingly; we didn't need to put on the heavy winter shooting clothes. Roughly about 5.30 a.m. on the first morning we went into the kitchen and to our surprise our guide had already prepared coffee, tea and toast for us; it was very much appreciated and not at all what we were used to. He had also prepared flasks, even down to a small hip flask filled with brandy for later; what a guy he was. He didn't know much about goose shooting but he certainly was an excellent host.

The Range Rover was ready with nets and decoys; he must have put them in the previous night. He did have some very nice shell goose decoys but they didn't look like they'd had much field work. We also suggested that he remove his green nets as our desert camo ones would be a better choice for the morning on the stubble field.

Once on the field we placed the decoys, all fifty of them and erected the hides, it was then a simple matter of just sitting and waiting for it to break light. We weren't sure what we would see, if anything, as the field we'd been on the previous afternoon had shown no signs of geese at all. The guide returned to sit and watch from his car which he had parked in the farm yard a good quarter of a mile away. We had the field to ourselves and as it began to break light it wasn't long before we heard Greylags calling in the distance.

It was just after eight thirty and we could see lots of geese in the distance but not many were coming our way. We tried calling but they were just not interested. Four large skeins went over us very high (like dots in the sky) and then a small bunch seemed to appear from nowhere and took us all by surprise. They had their wings set and were coming into towards the decoys very fast, dropping and spiralling out of the sky like bricks. Five birds were taken out in the first seven shots and one of them nearly hit me as it crashed into the fence next to me, skinning itself across its chest as it hit the top strand of barbed wire, at one almighty speed. Within a few minutes another small bunch came in but only two were shot but it wasn't from the lack of shots, just terrible shooting. Shortly after that a single bird committed the cardinal sin and came right into the decoys and caller. We had taken eight birds in fifteen minutes and it looked like it could be an amazing morning. But it wasn't to be, it was all over; no more geese. We hung on as long as we could but nothing else came near us. We sat in the warm sunshine until just short of ten o'clock when a few thousand came right over the top of us but they were so high an anti-aircraft gun couldn't have reached them. Coming across the field as fast as he could, was the guide shouting loudly out of the car window. "Look boys, ten o'clock, pointing at his watch, didn't I tell you." Well, we all had a laugh but we were not complaining as we had shot geese and still had a few days of shooting left.

Once back at the cabin it was a quick wash, shower and change before breakfast and what a breakfast it was. In all my years of shooting and staying in hotels this breakfast beat all others. It was one of the best breakfasts we had ever experienced and it filled us so much that all we wanted was a sleep to recover from it. We certainly were getting great value for our money especially on the high standard of food.

It was suggested we try and get a few geese and ducks that evening; they usually came into a small loch very close to where we had been shooting that morning. It may have been the very same geese we had seen in the morning and they may have been coming off that small loch. We weren't too keen on shooting birds coming back into roost for the evening but with the amount of geese in that area it's doubtful we would have done much harm. With the weather being so mild and calm without a breath of wind it could turn out to be a total disaster and may not be worth going out at all, plus it was also about a half moon.

That afternoon we did have a siesta as having a very late night and early morning we were shattered and that amazing breakfast had finished us off totally. The guide decided to go for a ride to see where the geese were feeding to make sure we would get a crack at them the next morning. We were invited to join him but a sleep was needed to bring us back to full speed once again.

At about three o'clock we travelled down a long narrow lane which led us to a small loch in the middle of a very large stubble field. There was virtually no cover at all around it, just a wire fence running lengthways, possibly ten yards off the water's edge. No bushes, no hedges, nothing to get into or hide behind. It certainly didn't look very promising. The loch was about two hundred and fifty yards in length and about eighty yards across. I didn't fancy lying flat on wet grass until it became dark enough to kneel up and hopefully get some shots.(trying to hide behind a fence post is nigh on impossible) We all felt the same and wondered how on earth we were going to shoot it. After speaking to the guide he told us that the loch had never been shot before and he wasn't sure what would come in, if anything and he certainly hadn't been feeding it, why would he? We had expected to be sitting in nice comfortable hides and felt there was something not quite right. The guide also told us that we must not cross over the fence and to stay on one side only which was very strange indeed, especially when the estate owned all the land and farms in that area. We sat a few hundred yards back, amongst some large round bales that had been left on the field and waited for the light to start fading. Then, as it went little bit darker we were told by the guide to move up and get closer to the fence line which was close to the water's edge. Even at dusk we stood out like sore thumbs so much so that anything coming into that loch would have certainly seen us far too easily. After about another thirty minutes of lying down the best we could we heard Widgeon and geese starting to move. We did get a few Mallard flying over the loch at a great height but they didn't look or come anywhere near us; obviously going elsewhere.

As it grew darker we were able to sit up a little. A bunch of Greylags came over quite low and circled to make their approach but were more towards the top of the loch. We did have a gun placed there and as the birds were just about to touch down there was an almighty BOOM and the sky lit up with flashes like fireworks going off. The gun had used some home loaded black powder cartridges and with no wind what-so-ever the smoke was hanging over the loch like smog. All we heard was," did I get anything"? It was so funny because when he had pulled the trigger the smoke had completely

A Wild Goose Chase

blocked out his vision. As it happened he had pulled out a Greylag but all we could hear, was him chuntering and complaining about the smoke.

It was now much darker and right on the flight time when the guide shouted from a distance. "Right boys you can get over the fence and get closer if you would like to." Quite a few Widgeon and geese were missed that evening, our bag was only two Greylags but it was not for the lack of trying. No one seemed to be on good form that evening. It could well have been because of all the smoke hanging over the water, anyway that was our excuse. After the flight had finished our pal certainly took quite a bit of flak from us. Why on earth was he using black powder home loads? We told him "NEVER AGAIN." I doubt he will ever live it down. Black powder home loads on a loch, I ask you. Boy did he get it off us but it did give us something to talk about that night.

Earlier in the book I mentioned shooting with a Polish keeper on a farm in the Crief area and the farmer had mentioned he owned a loch a few miles away. Well, we found out a few years later that this was the one we had just been shooting. The guide certainly didn't have permission to shoot on it what-so-ever. No wonder he kept us back until it was quite dark because we were poaching.

One afternoon we did manage a walk about on the pheasants and shot really well, we saw a great number of them but

A Wild Goose Chase

looking back I often wonder if we were poaching them also. Did they also belong to the other farmer? Anyway we never did find out but getting quite a few Pheasant certainly increased our bag.

One evening the guide received a phone call just as we were having our meal and it didn't sound very good at all. He was talking in a very loud voice, promising to do something about the problem and said he would be straight there after his evening meal and would sort it. He wasn't happy, to say the least, when he came off the phone and told us that Red Deer had strayed into a kale field and the farmer was playing holy hell with him. He asked if we would go with him and give him a hand; now that's an offer not to refuse.

When we arrived at the field it was very dark as the moon was obscured by heavy, dark clouds. The guide got very quietly out of the Rover and we were told not to make any sound at all whilst getting out. He passed powerful hand held search lights to two of us and told us not do anything until he said NOW. We then had to switch them both on, pointing towards the kale field. It was very exciting and a bit nerve wracking because we hadn't a clue where we were, never mind how many deer there were.

The guide was very safety conscious and made sure we were positioned in the right place before he took out and rested his rifle and tripod on the car bonnet. He asked if we were ready and asked us to keep the lights on the deer at all times, even if they started running. The excitement was getting to us and the adrenalin was certainly flowing as he gave the instruction to switch on the lights. The field lit up; there were red deer everywhere, Stags and Hinds, about sixty yards from us. There must have been over a hundred Red Deer, startled and frozen to the spot by our search lights. Within a split second he dropped one like a brick. He stood up and free standing, took another shot at one as it ran away. It dropped, stone dead, with its legs buckling underneath it and rolling head over heels before becoming motionless. He may have not known much about goose shooting but he certainly was one hell of a shot on the deer. We stood there looking at him in total amazement and disbelief at what we had just seen. 'Annie Oakley eat your heart out.' All he said was "that should keep the little shits off this field for a few days" He Gralloched them, right there on the field before putting the two young stag carcasses in the back of the Rover and boy did they stink. But that was to be expected, it was October and the Rut was on. The skin smelled strongly of urine and of wallowing in smelly peat bogs, getting ready for the mating season. Ugh...

Our holiday came to an end with a good bag, a number of Greylags, a few Pinks and Pheasants, plus two haunches of Venison and not forgetting some Red Deer antlers, we didn't have any complaints at all really. The accommodation, hospitality and food were out of this world and not expensive by any standards.

We didn't go back again and I often wonder how he got on with the other goose shooting parties. Did they actually believe him about the worm casts, (where the geese put their beaks when sleeping) and whether or not he took them onto the same loch to shoot ducks and geese, knowing full well he was poaching?

Westmorland Wildfowlers

For many years I was dedicated to wild fowling on the local marshes near Kendal, Cumbria, which was then part of Westmorland. My wild fowling days were probably my first experiences of sitting knee deep in a gutter. I would head out onto the marshes at 'silly o clock' in the morning, in freezing and difficult conditions but perfect for wild fowling. Looking back it gave me vast amounts of knowledge and experience for the foreshore and inland goose shooting that was to follow. The club I was a member of was very well run and still is and offered some excellent opportunities to flight Mallard, Geese, Widgeon, Teal, Golden Eye, Pintail and many other types of wild fowl.

We used to go onto the marshes regularly, mainly for the morning flights as they were only fifteen minutes away by car. I would also nip down occasionally after work, if the weather conditions were favourable for an evening flighting. Being a Stone Mason, it was great in the winter months when the strong winds and rain prevented me from working; it gave me much more time for wildfowling and marsh shooting.

The club have always done a great job with regard to conservation and invested time and money to create a place to be enjoyed by many. Now and again we would encounter photographers who loved taking photos of all the different types of birds. It was a haven for wild birds during the winter months and offered good shelter for the migrating wildfowl to feed and rest before moving on. 'Twitchers' used to have a go at us regularly about shooting. They were soon put right, if it wasn't for the time and money the local wild fowlers invested to help create a better habitat for the birds then there wouldn't be many to watch and photograph. One of my favourite replies was; may I ask how much money you have invested into making this area better for the birds? That usually did the trick but I just wish people would listen and understand and not judge, calling us callous, non-caring murderers.

I personally enjoyed the tide flights as it gave many opportunities to have a crack at the different types of ducks as they moved further inwards to get away from the incoming and racing tide. The tide on the estuary is known for its speed, especially when it's a high one, it can come in so fast it creates a bore; a bore to be scared of. Knowledge of all the marshes was very important and many lives have been lost by unsuspecting visitors taking unnecessary risks. It is also very well known for dangerous quicksand and over the years I'd managed to get stuck in them on a few occasions and having to pull my feet out of my waders to get myself free and out of danger.

I had many, many, flights on those marshes but one that always springs to mind is the one when the tide was due to start running at around the same time it was going to break light. That is one of the best tides to get the birds to move, after a long overnight rest. Hopefully, they would move onto the marshes; it was going to be one heck of a chance to get amongst the ducks. The marsh I frequented had some deep gutters so keeping hidden wasn't a problem and they were just perfect to keep Blackie well-hidden also. From the car park to where I was going was only a ten minute walk and didn't pose many problems for me to reach my favourite gutter; on the very edge of the sands.

It was the second week in January and there had been a severe frost overnight and there had also been a slight dusting of snow. I've always loved the sound of ice cracking under foot whilst walking across the marshes and your breath being visible; as your pace increased.

Years ago there weren't any thermal or neoprene waders to keep your feet warm and I always hated having to put them on after getting out of a warm car. They always felt so cold but soon warmed up as you began walking, getting the blood flow going. My favourite jacket was the good old Barbour wax proof. It was so stiff to put on especially if it had been wet a few days before or left in the boot of the car without letting it dry out properly.

I used to be a smoker and once I was settled in the gutter it would be a quick ciggie and a scan with the glasses to see if I could glimpse any movement on the incoming tide. As usual when it did start to break light the temperature dropped dramatically and I often heard and felt Blackie shivering. He would sneak up to me and snuggle under the bottom of my open jacket to keep himself warm. However, if I did shoot a duck or goose he would be out into the water without any hesitation, whatsoever.

Curlews, Gulls and lots of other birds were getting restless so I scanned once again; looking way out into the estuary. There was lots of movement so the tide must have started to run.

Blackie who was my eyes in a morning, especially at the break of dawn always let me know when something was coming. He would stand and look up; I should have called him Radar because he missed nothing. He wasn't a well-trained dog he just loved being on those marshes with me; we certainly had a very strong bond together for many happy years. Taking him on a Pheasant shoot would have been disastrous because he would probably have flushed and chased anything that moved and stopping him, well, I doubt he would have stopped because he ran in to most things. I never blamed him as he was my first ever gundog and I hadn't a clue how to train one. But on the marshes he came into his own and just wanted to please me all the time by bringing the shot birds back to me and it was always to hand. He knew those marshes like the back of his tail and if he ever heard geese I had to hold him back because he became so excited. He definitely had 'Goose Fever'

The first birds to come over me were Curlews and in those days they could be legally shot but I let them through because I was waiting for the Mallard and Widgeon. The flight of Curlews went on for ages there were hundreds and hundreds of them. It was then that a pair of Mallard whizzed over my head without me even seeing them and Blackie was looking at me as if to say, why didn't you shoot? My first chance and I was caught napping.

The tide was now moving very quickly and the ducks were flying just ahead of it, it was pushing them closer to the edge of the marsh which was very near to where we lay hidden. I was only about fifteen yards away from the sand, well concealed and ready. A few shots went off from behind me about a mile away on a different marsh; the flight had started.

I had a lot of shots that morning mainly at Widgeon but for some reason I just wasn't connecting well with them. Blackie did a great job retrieving four but the tide was now racing in and the gutter was starting to fill up very quickly indeed. We moved back to a safer place and carried on shooting. It was a good flight and there were a great many ducks in the air. The sound of the Widgeon whistling was very encouraging... but just my luck they decided to follow the edge where we had been sitting earlier. The gutter now was so full it would have been impossible to have stayed; we could have drowned.

It was one of those frustrating mornings (but that's wild fowling) watching so many ducks in the air and wishing I'd been under them. They were flying very low, maybe only twenty yards up in the air; so easy to hit . I bet lots of fowlers have said similar and then missed the 'easy peasy ones.' (Smiles... because I know)

I was probably about three to four hundred yards away from all the action but it's nice just to sit and watch sometimes. I had four birds in my bag so I was more than happy.

After another fifteen minutes I decided to go back to the car. The flight was all but over and I was nowhere near the birds' flight line now. I was just putting my gun slip over my shoulder and packing my game bag when Blackie jumped out of the small gutter and stood up, looking with his head locked like a pointer, he always did this when he could see or hear something. I knelt down again and it was then I heard the sound of Greylags somewhere in the distance. I quickly reloaded three inch BB magnums into my Mossberg and slithered down as low as I could with Blackie pulled as close as possible into my side. There were about three skeins coming straight towards me from Brogden but still a long way off. My old heart was pounding and the hairs all over my body were standing straight up. I tried to hide myself the best I could resisting any sudden movement but I could feel water trickling down inside my waders; it was freezing and the tide was filling the gutter very quickly.

They came right over me about thirty yards up and I took three shots without touching a single feather. I was absolutely gutted asking myself, what the hell am I doing wrong this morning? I sat on the grass in total disbelief and just to top the morning off completely, I had forgotten about the wet salt grass so I finished up with a soggy bottom as well.

Once again Blackie was staring at me looking totally disgusted. As we made our way back to the car he ran off ahead of me and wouldn't stop. It was fairly normal for him so I didn't think too much of it really but suddenly he reappeared with a Greylag held firmly in his mouth. I had no idea it had dropped out after my shots but Blackie did and I often wondered if he was trying to tell me something when we were in the gutter. I will never know but good job Blackie, he was a cracking fowling dog.

Blackie: 'a cracking fowling dog'

Dunning Perthshire

Dunning in Perthshire is an endearing old village, snuggled in the Ochils in beautiful Strathearn. It was next door to Rats Paradise which is situated in the Forteviot area. It's only a small place and we found this bit of shooting by mistake one day whilst taking a wrong turn. (We were rubbish at map reading.)

It was one of those beautiful, sunny, late autumn, afternoons and we were making our way towards Perthshire when I spotted what looked like skeins of geese descending into some fields a few miles north of us. We had never been on that particular road before and it wasn't long before we were driving through the small village of Dunning. We pulled over and went into the local shop to get a few supplies; it was there that I met a local farmer. He stood outside the shop just staring at me in my shooting gear; he walked over and asked. "Are you shooters"? I replied, "We sure are." I hadn't a clue who he was, in-fact I wasn't too sure where we were either but I did know we weren't too far from our normal shooting grounds.

A Wild Goose Chase

It turned out he was expecting a shooting party a few days prior but they hadn't turned up. He asked if we would shoot some geese for him; they were making such a mess on one of his potato fields. We followed him back to the farm and realised it was where we had seen the geese in the distance, earlier that day. How lucky could we get, what a great opportunity. We shot on that farm for many years but it was during a conversation at home one evening with a neighbour that brought me to this chapter of the book. He wanted to have a shot at goose.

It was suggested that four of us would travel through the early hours of the morning taking our time for a change. Setting off around midnight would give us plenty of time to arrive at the farm by six o'clock. I'd already contacted the farmer and he told me that there were plenty of geese around. We packed the gear and set off just after midnight and of course had our usual stop at Hamilton Services for a full English Monty. We arrived early and decided to have a look around. I was able to drive across a very large stubble field and located the potato field where we would be shooting. As soon as we stopped we grabbed torches; put wellies or boots on and surveyed the field and found it was completely covered in goose muck. It sure did look like the newbies with us would get some goose shooting.

The excitement was electric and as usual there was lots of banter. We certainly weren't in a rush to get the decoys out or erect the two hides. We unloaded the car and I drove it back to the farm and put it in one of the barns, well out of sight.

Blackie's life had ended quite a few years prior and I now had a three year old Golden Labrador called Purdy. I'd had her since she was seven weeks old and she was trained to a good standard; not at all like Blackie. She was good at most things, especially retrieving geese. To her it was easy, plus she didn't have the dreaded 'goose fever'. She would lay anywhere and not move until she was asked, a very placid and well behaved dog; just for a change.

The hides were erected and blended in very well; even I had difficulty seeing them. If I couldn't see them there was no chance the birds would. It was just a matter of time now before we would, hopefully, be shooting geese. I was in the hide with Alan (my best mate) and Darren and Steele were about twenty yards from us on an opposite fence line; they blended in so perfectly in fact it was very difficult to see them at all.

As it was getting lighter we could see headlights and hear vehicles from the neighbouring farm. Two vehicles came onto the field but away from our boundary; shining very powerful spotlights all over the field. I wondered if it was some of my other friends who'd decided to drive up and have

A Wild Goose Chase

a go at the geese after finding out about the numbers in the area.

We could hear geese shouting in the distance but whoever this was they would have to get a spurt on or they would ruin the early part of the flight. They had two trailers full of decoys and three hides were soon placed fairly close together (about ten yards apart).They put out loads of decoys in front of the hides but also behind as well. We realised then that it wasn't our friends, but who was it? Seven guns went into the hides and the Land Rovers were taken away, well out of sight. We watched in total disbelief, some of them were running around the field fooling around with the decoys like big kids. The geese were now airborne and getting closer, coming towards us. We shouted and whistled at the other shooters but they couldn't hear us because of the distance between us.

The first line of Pinks came in to our ten decoys, they never faltered and two birds were easily taken, I think nerves got the better of us because a number of geese were missed. The sky was full of skeins making their way towards us. There was a slight breeze and this made geese go around the bottom of the field and then make their final, well calculated approach towards us; clambering and sounding very noisy. They were about two hundred yards from us when they changed direction, turning towards the other shooters decoys. They went straight in; it sounded like the Alamo, with the number of shots going off.

Every gun must have been using an auto and each gun was emptying out. It was sheer carnage watching those unsuspecting geese get hammered. One very hard hit bird went out over the field and then back again over the guns, taking at least ten more shots before finally dropping but still wounded. Alan and I sat there in utter disgust watching the brutality taking place. More birds went into their guns and again there was no mercy, birds were dropping all over the field. No one was bothering to pick them up, leaving wounded birds to walk off, probably in severe pain. The number of shots was contemptible, at one point there were towards thirty shots in one barrage with only one bird dropping out of the skein. Many birds drifted away pricked but again no one bothered to retrieve them.

Some Pinks came into us; we managed to shoot nine and decided it was time to pack up; nearly all the other skeins went into the other shooters. I'm certainly not against big bags being taken but this was beyond sense or reason. It was slaughter at its best and made us feel sick inside.

Darren, Steele and my good friend Alan

We packed up and watched through the glasses as they continued to slaughter the geese. In all my years of shooting geese I have never seen anything so barbaric in my life. I went to bring the car; our two guests had thoroughly enjoyed the shooting but had also been sickened by the other shooting team; witnessing a no mercy killing of some of the most magnificent birds alive.

They shot until ten o'clock and had probably taken well over a hundred birds; not counting the un-picked ones. A person with a dog was making his way across the stubble field towards us, a good three hundred yards away, to retrieve a wounded goose. It gave me a hell of an opportunity to see who it was slaughtering the geese. I wasn't in the best of moods by then and I was certain it would lead to something more than just an exchange of words. I jumped over the fence followed swiftly by Purdy and made my way quickly towards him.

I was stunned when I realised who it was, I had known him for a good many years. "Good flight Mike"? He said. I cannot and will not type what I said in return but it had stunned me, more because I knew the person fairly well and for a long time. I let fly verbally with everything I had and told him he should be totally ashamed of himself for taking so many geese, never mind the wounded ones that still hadn't been picked. I also told him he was an utter disgrace to shooting.

After my tirade and I'd calmed down a little he told me that the group were Italian and were paying a lot of money to shoot. I remember clearly something I did say to him, "you're going to *uck up goose shooting completely by greed alone. He just laughed and said "It's my living so I will let them do what they want". That was when charges for goose shooting started to come into being; many more people began charging to take guests out to shoot the geese.

My 'so called friend' was even on the farm where we used to shoot (Rats Paradise) and had offered the farmer an extortionate amount of money for permission to bring shooters on a regular basis. Many of these shooters were Italian who were willing to pay ridiculous amounts of money and that's when it all started to go wrong.

I told him what I thought of him whilst he was busy trying to get his dog to go out about a hundred yards to pick up a wounded goose. A goose which could be seen very easily. He tried and tried to get his dog to go to pick it up, in the end I asked Purdy once and off she went like a rocket. I could hear a cheer come from our lads in the distant field; they had been watching everything. When she brought it back I took it off her and walked away, half expecting an argument but nothing was said, he just walked away chuntering. No way was I giving him that bird.

That day was one of the worst days I've ever experienced when out goose shooting. There weren't any bag limits then and there were no restrictions on how many shells you could put in your gun and of course lead was allowed. But surely common sense should always prevail. I once found a heap of dead geese left under a hedgerow to rot; which wasn't a very pleasant experience. How could anyone do that? It's awful to see and I could sense it was all going to change. Goose shooting would never be the same again.

It wasn't long after that many more shooters travelled to Scotland to shoot the geese. Large sums of money were being offered to the farmers for exclusive rights and I certainly wasn't in any position to challenge them. It is true 'money is the root of all evil'.

One farmer friend told me that he could make a fortune while sat in his croft through the winter months. He wasn't bothered who shot the geese. They made such a mess of his land he was glad to be rid of them and he received a steady, regular, income which helped him tremendously. Oh and going back to the Italians who did the slaughter; would you believe that when I went over to see if they had cleaned up the field properly I found over 100 empty cartridges and quite a lot of them were number 6's. How disgusting is that?

Alan - My Best Mate

For many years I helped a keeper friend of mine to put in rabbit netting to protect new plantings. I regularly helped him and one of the perks was being given permission to shoot the pigeons in the woods and on the stubble fields, I was also able to help him on his Pheasant shoot. This particular day I was introduced to the rabbit catcher and his son Alan. The family had moved from Yorkshire to work for the local estate and were given an estate cottage in the centre of Whinfell Forest. The cottage was fairly isolated but stood in a small clearing surrounded by woodland; it was a quiet but beautiful place to live. The forest where Alan and his family lived is now the leisure park called 'Centre Parks' near Penrith, Cumbria. Alan was around thirteen when we met that day and I didn't see him again until he was in his early twenties and we have been the best of pals since. That's now over thirty years and boy oh boy could we write a few stories about our escapades.

Alan spent most of his early years training as a keeper and has been a keeper in the area all his adult life. He is now working as Lord Lonsdale's Head Keeper. It's not a large shoot but offers guns a few driven birds, put over them or small groups who get together to have a walk about the estate and enjoy some rough shooting. The estate offers some superb wild Pheasants and of course the unsuspecting Woodcock which nearly always take the guns by surprise. Alan and I have always got on extremely well and have had some outstanding days shooting over the years especially amongst the crows, pigeons and foxes, plus keeping all the other types of vermin controlled. There are far too many stories to write about but some I would like to share, mainly goose shooting but a few in other areas.

Greylags have been in the Penrith area for a number of years but never in great numbers. It's taken many years to build up the stock a level where some can be shot under controlled conditions and imposed bag limits were brought in to protect them. It has certainly paid dividends and each year the numbers increase because of the tremendous work Alan does ensuring their numbers continue to grow. When Alan first started I doubt there would have been a hundred local Greylags but now there must be fifteen hundred, probably more towards the two thousand mark. If that's not testimony of good conservation and protection then nothing is, 'one in the eye' for the anti-shooters.

When the birds come onto the stubble in September it's a sight and sound not to be missed, shooters love it. The way these birds are shot is slightly different from most types of goose shooting. The Greylags in this area normally come into the stubble an hour or so before dusk. They nip in; have a feed then return to the safety of their roosting waters.

If you would like to see some clips go onto YouTube and type in *tewka2003* it will take you to some of the shooting videos I have put together over the years. But, please remember I'm just a novice so don't expect a BBC documentary.

It's a tremendous sight to see, the shooters tucked into the hides with their shell decoys in position. Alan and I sit back and watch from a distance, keeping in touch with them via walkie-talkies. Sometimes I sit a little bit away from them, in my stealth suit, hidden completely hoping to do a bit of videoing. Watching others get a chance of shooting a goose is just as exciting for me; I have had that opportunity many, many times before. Many of the groups we take out have never had wild geese coming into them or ever shot a goose before. The after talk is always very interesting to listen to, a full analysis of why, what and how they should have shot; but nearly all the groups get their bag limit of four geese per gun. We aim to get the bag limit and get off the field as quickly as possible to let the other geese settle back in.

Alan being the keeper has allowed me to get more involved with other shooters and for a number of years has organised many very successful driven pheasant shoots. The one he's employed on now is Towcett Estate; it's a small friendly shoot allowing small groups to shoot. Careful management and excellent vermin control have made the shoot flourish in many ways.

Although I have done a great deal of goose shooting, if I was to be honest with myself I think pigeon shooting would be my first love simply because of the amount of shots you can get in a day when its busy with the Pigeons. Every spring on the drilling and every late summer Alan and I are out decoying the pigeons and crows. With the pigeons it's the speed and the challenge they offer plus with the amount of birds it could keep us busy for a full afternoon of decoying.

The Penrith area isn't the same as other areas because we don't get massive amounts of pigeons but we have shot over a hundred between us on stubble fields or fresh drilling and had a cracking day.

On one occasion I received a call from Alan early in the morning asking if I would like a day on the pigeons. It was going to be difficult, my wife was in hospital recovering from a serious knee operation and I was looking after my son Simon who was only five years old. On top of that Purdy (my Labrador) was still only a puppy. It took only a few seconds thought for me to decide. It didn't take much thinking about at all really and Alan said Simon would probably love it. But my young pup I wasn't too sure about, she had never sat in a hide before but to miss an opportunity like that would have been sacrilege.

We drove to the farm to let the farmer know we would be shooting on one of his fields that afternoon but he laughed whole heartedly saying, 'you're wasting your time lads the barley's been treated and the pigeons won't touch it.' "BUGGER" we said, to each other but we'll go and look anyway.

To our total surprise there must have been over five hundred birds' already merrily feeding, heads bobbing up and down in unison. It was one of those moments where we wondered if the farmer was just winding us up. The pigeons didn't seem bothered at all about eating that freshly drilled, treated, barley seed. The problem was where do we put the hide with birds all over the field? After watching the flight line for a short while and many new birds joining the others we decided to go to the top of the field. We would put the hide up against a bit of wall that was just and so visible from where we were. At least we would be looking downwards with a full view of the entire field. It was a good vantage point and we would be able to see any change in the pigeons' movements enabling us to move positions easily, if necessary.

Simon helped to position the decoys whilst Alan took the vehicle away. Purdy was enjoying every minute, and picking up the new scent of pigeon. We sat in front of a wall about four yards in length; it wasn't high and had an old dead Blackthorn bush on the end. It was a perfect position for the afternoons shooting once the hide was in place. This was Simon's first time out with me shooting pigeons and I would have to keep Purdy controlled as she was far too young to retrieve pigeons and I wouldn't want loose pigeon feathers getting stuck in her throat and choking her.

The usual thing with shooters is once everything is set up, to relax a bit and have a brew but this time it didn't happen because it started within minutes. Pigeons were coming in from every direction and dropping into the decoys from a great height, chests out, wings tucked in and dropping in like bricks. I'm convinced that even if I'd had a bright red shirt on it wouldn't have made any difference; they ignored us completely. My biggest worry was keeping an eye on Purdy and she did get somewhat excited but she did manage and remained fairly still and never once ran out of the hide. I hit a bird and wounded it and was about to go and get it when Simon asked if he could go instead. We let him go and watched as he chased it, caught it, dispatched it and placed it in the decoy pattern, ever so carefully, tucking its wings in and removing any loose feathers. He returned into the hide very excited and said "I straggled it Dad. I straggled it"

Alan and I had a bit of a laugh and it was then I realised he was not going to have any problem shooting. He was a natural without a doubt and nothing seemed to faze him even at such a young age. Boy oh boy did they keep coming, flocks of up to thirty birds at times and our shooting wasn't too bad either. There was a constant movement of pigeons all afternoon and the shot noise didn't bother them one bit. Purdy was made redundant as we had found our new retriever (Simon) who wanted to go out and get the birds, placing them perfectly in amongst the decoys. I kept an eye on Purdy but she was doing amazingly well and didn't need tethering once, she had the makings of a good gun dog. I wouldn't let her carry any pigeons but let her have a good sniff at them. I didn't actually need her; Simon was taking over her job completely. As he was retrieving yet another bird Alan burst out laughing and said," You remember the first pigeon Simon straggled." I replied, "Yes. Why"? He said, "Look." and I could see a pigeon waddling off looking rather bedraggled with hardly any feathers left on its neck. We had a good chuckle over it and quickly despatched it. It came up in shooting conversations for years afterwards. Sy is now in his early thirties and we still pull his leg about it, (and how he straggled his first pigeon)

My young son Sy on the Pigeons

At one stage in the afternoon Alan had to nip back to the car for more cartridges and once again the pigeons kept coming. The total for our days shooting was one hundred and forty three pigeons and a couple of Carrion crows. Not bad at all by any standard but for us that was a lot of birds. Our average bags would be in the region of twenty to thirty, to get well over a hundred was far beyond our expectations.

The day ended on a high, a good number of pigeons, steady puppy and a new retriever called Simon.

To have Simon and Purdy do so well was the icing on the cake for me. I was looking forward to all the times ahead, father and son and best friend Alan together shooting; with of course Purdy who was by far the best dog I ever had.

A Wild Goose Chase

It Could Only Happen To Me

As you're probably well aware by now I have chased geese all over Scotland; inland shooting was mainly in the North East whilst foreshore shooting was on the North West coast. At times we would venture further afield, up to the most northerly tip of Scotland but occasionally I was invited to go down south which always produced geese. Without doubt my trips north to the Isle of Bute and Islay were by far the best for the fabulous scenery.

My next story happened in a small town called Auchterarder, Scotland. Long before the commercial side of shooting hit the area; we had the pick of farms where we had permission to shoot and could go as often as wanted. It was just a quick phone call to the farmer, to check if the geese were there.

We booked into the Auchterarder Hotel for our usual three full days of goose shooting but as I was still employed by the shoe factory I could only go during the annual holiday week. We set off mid to late afternoon and arrived around seven o'clock after an uneventful journey, only stopping once to stretch our legs. We checked in, went to our rooms and dropped off our bags, deciding to unpack later as we were starving. We had a quick bite to eat and then off to find the fields where the geese had been feeding.

We decided to visit a farmer friend where we shot quite regularly; he would be a good source of information with regard to the whereabouts of the geese.

Jock Murrow and his wife Morag were such lovely people with 'hearts of gold' and we always called to see them even if we weren't shooting on their farm. Jock was a tenant farmer and worked very long hours producing oats, wheat and barley for large companies such as Dewar's Whisky. He had a very large acreage and would sometimes plant a single massive field of potatoes (red skins) which was great for attracting the geese. Jock also loved a wee dram or what he called a wee half of whisky and we always took him a bottle of 'the Low Flyer' (Grouse), nothing was ever too much trouble for Jock and Morag and they always made us feel very welcome.

As we approached the farm that evening we noticed it was in total darkness and wondered if Jock and Morag had decided to leave or if they had retired. Just as I was about to turn around and leave I noticed a little glimmer of light coming from a front window, it looked very much like candle light.

I knocked and it wasn't too long before he was stood in front of us in the doorway with the biggest, happiest smile on his face you could ever imagine. It was like meeting back up with a long lost buddy, he made us so welcome or was it because he knew we would have a bottle or two for him to enjoy. As we walked inside Morag came rushing through and gave us both a massive hug. She was an amazing and genuine lady and a real grafter.

There were candles of all shapes and sizes burning and food was being cooked on a wood burner type stove. The lovely smell of wood, burning in the air masked the smell of the many candles.

We sat for a while chatting like old friends do but as we readied to go Morag quickly asked us to sit back down and offered us some Stovies and a wee nip of whisky. She said it was to welcome us back and we had to make ourselves at home. I gave Jock two bottles of Grouse and gave both of them a pair of shoes each as a thank you gesture for letting us shoot on the land for the next three days.

The moon was rising and as it did the geese started moving very quickly, we could hear them clearly even though we were inside the croft. Jock explained to us that the geese had knocked out the electric cables yet again and he like so many other local farmers would have to wait until they left the area before being re-connected by the Scottish electricity board.

They would however receive some form of compensation which made him smile. Then came the fatal words, you will have a wee one with me boys? We did and another and another one until it warmed the cockles of the heart and we were beginning to glow.

Although we had just eaten at the hotel we had to sit with them and have a bowl of Stovies (it's something like scouse or corned beef ash) with lots of veggies and a few lumps of what I thought was Mutton.

He was telling us about the geese and how he was getting fed up with the damage they were doing to his fields. He kept a few sheep and set aside a couple of fields for them to graze but the geese had been on and stripped the grass right down. Because of all the goose muck he'd had to rent a field off a farmer friend for the sheep to graze; he wasn't a happy chappie at all.

It was about nine thirty and we had to drive back to the hotel, being laced with whisky was a definite No No for me. We tried our best to get out of yet another whisky but Jock insisted and said he would call his friends to pick us up and drive us back to the hotel later. That seemed fair enough and he arranged for them to come at midnight and drive us back in our car.

We talked mainly about families but chatted about all sorts sometimes quite in depth. They were lovely company but I could sense myself beginning to slur a little while speaking and desperately needed the toilet. I wasn't a big fan of whisky and only needed a couple before it had an effect on me. I decided to nip outside to relieve myself and grab some fresh air hoping it would sober me up a little. (They had an outside toilet, well a small tin shed really) It was then that I saw and heard the geese. They were dropping into a field next to the farm; hundreds of them shouting and squabbling. It was easy to see them flying and boy were they low, I raced back inside and suggested I might do a stalk on them a bit later. Jock thought I had lost the plot totally and couldn't really understand what I was talking about. All he said was, "why do you do that"? I just pick them up in the morning I don't have to shoot them. What the hell was he on about; I thought, too much drink must have fogged his senses.

Morag made me some very strong coffee and I began to feel much better so got my Zabala 10 bore side by side out of the car. I was convinced the stalk could be done as the field rose slightly and the geese were landing just over the top of it, I would be able to get fairly close to them without being seen.

Jock and my friend were well done after consuming even more drink and were having a very serious but very drunken conversation. I was lucky to have my waterproof Camo jacket with me but I only had denim jeans on and a pair of brogues but I was convinced I could get a shot or shots at the geese.

I sat and chatted to Morag as Jock and my pal chatted on and on having a good debate about farming and how things had changed over the years. They didn't even notice that I was about to leave the croft and try a stalk; they were totally engrossed and oblivious to anything else. Morag came outside with me, still a little confused with what I was going to do. She just shook her head and smiled at me and as she went back inside said, "Just lift the latch when you get back Mike".

I stood at the boundary fence of the field and watched the birds' movements for a few minutes, watching how they were approaching before going in to land. I would have to stalk or crawl on my belly for at least two hundred yards to get anywhere near them, never mind get a shot at them. I set off with great intent and thought it would be a fantastic start to our shooting break if I was to bag a few that evening. Slowly, I made my way, on my belly, closer towards them; foot by foot. I had birds fly over me only twenty foot above but I couldn't roll over fast enough and mount the gun in time before they were gone. I was so tempted to have a go but decided I was going for the stalk instead. I was getting closer to the top of the hill and the noise was getting louder and louder, there must have been hundreds just out in front of me. I heard a lot of geese coming in from behind me, I rolled over and had the 10 bore ready when they sussed me and started calling very loudly and 'back flying', using their alarm calls to warn the others, their wings rattling loudly right above me. There was a deathly silence from the other geese for a few seconds, the alarm call had worked well, suddenly there was an almighty roar which grew in intensity as a few thousand geese became airborne in a mad noisy panic. That was it; I had spooked them completely and didn't get a single shot at them. A massive black cloud of geese could be seen silhouetted flying away into the distance, getting as far away from me as they possibly could.

I arrived back at the croft, completely sober by this time and quite disheartened. I lifted the latch to go inside and I could hear Jock and my pal still laughing. Morag was in hysterics over something so I assumed she must have joined them and had a whisky or two. I told them in great detail what had happened but my friend had had far too many whiskeys to be remotely interested. Jock poured me another very large whiskey and repeated what he had said earlier in the evening, "just go out in the morning and pick a few up like I do." "What do you mean by that Jock" I asked, "I don't understand." He looked at me again quite bemused and quietly told me that he had seven gin traps set out in the field and yes it was the very same field I had just belly crawled over. I remember a whisky going down rapidly and the blood draining from my face as I became very white (A Whiter

Shade of Pale) I had just stalked a field that had gin traps set out for the geese. My mind started imaging all sorts of what might or could have happened but phewww I still had my hands and feet. Never again did I go on Jock's land before finding out if he had any traps set out.

Around midnight two of Jock's friends came in a Land Rover, as promised and took us both back to the hotel; one of them drove our car back for us. Morag insisted we take some Stovies with us, she said it would help to sober up my friend ready for the morning. It was one hell of a night but I will always remember Morag and "Don't forget you're Stovies" (smiles). I very much doubt Jock would remember us being there after he and my friend downed nearly two bottles of Grouse. My friend had a hell of a hang-over next day but I hadn't involved myself too heavily, just the thought of belly crawling amongst gin traps was enough to sober anyone up. They were lovely down to earth people but yet again as more and more people came goose shooting they also were very much in favour of what they could make through the winter months without having to do a thing. Sad but it was starting to happen all over that area.

A Wild Goose Chase

The Blue Peter Hotel

For many years my wife, Jaqui and I ran a very successful business supplying garages and hauliers with specialist automotive cleaning products but after a long discussion we decided it was maybe time to sell, move on and look for something a little bit less stressful. We had been working seven days a week for many years and had not had a holiday together for twenty years, apart from my few snatched days each year with pals on goose shooting trips, which had become less and less over the years because of our business commitments.

We really fancied taking over a small hotel where we could offer golfing holidays for the summer months and goose shooting and rough shooting throughout the winter months. Finding somewhere to accommodate our plans was very difficult indeed and we had many trips looking at places without any success.

An advertising company informed us about a very small hotel for sale in a place called Kirkcolm which was situated on the

A Wild Goose Chase

West coast of Scotland and only a few miles from Stranraer. We decided to have a look at the place as it was an area I knew fairly well. I had been goose shooting on Stairs Estate many years before and knew that the geese would spend the winter months in the area. The drive along that part of the coast was very spectacular with some very stunning scenery, passing places like Luce Bay. We weren't convinced that we would find a hotel that could offer what we wanted but it was worth a look.

When we arrived at Stranraer we had a look round the port which was very pretty and then had a wander through the town, which is basically one main street. Lock Ryan looked quite picturesque as the HSS Voyager was making its way out of the port and heading towards Belfast, Northern Ireland. One of the things I can remember quite clearly was seeing Palm trees along the side of the port and how amazingly blue the sea looked.

We eventually arrived in the village of Kirkcolm which is situated on the coastline of Loch Ryan and about a ten to fifteen minute drive from Stranraer. The road through the village had houses either side and the hotel was situated approximately half way up the village, on the right hand side. There was no visible hotel car park so we sat in a small car park opposite the village shop looking at the hotel, 'The Blue Peter Hotel'. We sat and stared in disbelief, it looked a bit grim and not very well presented, in fact it looked very dismal and in a bad state of repair and we had just travelled four hours to look at it.

The Blue Peter Hotel

Once inside we were shown around and it didn't get any better. It stank of stale beer and nicotine dripped down the walls in the public bar. There was also a strong pungent smell of urine emanating from the nearby toilets. The lounge bar was an improvement but didn't look as if it had been used much at all; it was dark and dingy. The bar of the lounge was in the shape of a boat to give it a nautical theme and actually looked quite nice.

The hotel had three floors; the ground floor was taken up by an entrance hall, public bar, lounge bar and the toilets. The entrance hall led onto an open staircase leading to the second floor which had three on suite bedrooms, two doubles and a family room. On the same floor was large residents' lounge, the kitchen and owners private bathroom. The top floor was the owner's private accommodation and consisted of a lounge, and three bedrooms with a separate toilet.

The previous owners wanted to return back to England and be closer to their family and they hadn't had much interest in the hotel for at least three years. This was very apparent from the decoration, the whole place was filthy and the carpets, sticky and threadbare. The figures from the bar and accommodation weren't very encouraging either but this would be to our advantage when it came to discussing the purchase price. It was also a free-hold hotel which meant there were no ties to a particular brewery. This was a plus because breweries are always willing to inject money if their beers are being promoted. The hotel was in a great area for me with regard to shooting and there were three well known golf courses very close by.

We thought long and hard and after many discussions and arguments for and against we put a plan together and decided to go ahead. We put our house up for sale and in July 1997 we became the proud owners of The Blue Peter Hotel.

The first year was fun but very long hours and extremely hard work; between us we began to give the hotel a full make over. The locals started coming in and the bar and accommodation figures started to improve.

Being such a small village, of course, everyone knew their neighbours for miles around. It didn't take too long before the word had spread that I was looking to rent land for shooting from local farmers.

To cut to the chase towards the end of our first year I had obtained shooting rights on four farms where I knew the geese would come in the winter months. The farms were within ten minutes of the hotel and that was the icing on the cake, I was able to release around five hundred pheasants and five hundred ducks onto the same farms. Things were looking up for us; we were a golfing, fishing and shooting hotel. I even had a Blue Peter badge designed depicting a silhouette of a golfer, shooter and fisherman and round the edge it read, 'Been there and done that at the Blue Peter Hotel'. All the monies received from those badges went into a jar for a Christmas treat for the O.A.P's in the village.

One of our groups

I also obtained permission to shoot on a three thousand acre farm near Sandhead (he was English which helped). He cultivated mainly wheat and barley but was also well aware of how things worked regarding the charges for shooting. He wanted ten pounds per gun per flight but only if the guns shot, no shots and there wouldn't be a charge. This was a massive opportunity for me and we agreed I would have the shooting rights for three years. Knowing the area well I was aware that there were always large numbers of geese on that land during the winter shooting months; mainly Pinkfeet but with a possibility of a few Greylags.

I also obtained permission to shoot on Ardwell Estate and became good friends with the Keeper who offered to help me with any shooting parties if I was busy.

Jaqui had arranged excellent discounts with the three local golf courses and put together a three day package from March to September to include, three rounds of golf on three fantastic courses, meals and accommodation for only £99.00. I would take out fishing parties throughout the summer months fishing for Pollock and would also look after my Pheasants and young ducks.

The following summer we were fully booked with golfers and I had bookings for the shooting advertising via my website and also advertising through a few of the larger shooting magazines. Things were really looking up. Our second year had started and I had filled every available shooting date possible but how on earth was I going to be able to do it by myself? In winter I would organise and take out the shooting parties and throughout the summer Jaqui would be in charge of the golfing groups; together we made a fantastic team. We worked extremely long hours, the bar was open for guests until very late; eventually we had to take on staff, but that's another story.

Being in a small village meant we didn't have to be open through the day, the locals came in the evenings and at weekends. It also meant we could carry out the majority of renovation work ourselves.

The hotel was beginning to look good, freshly painted and decorated with new carpets throughout.

Eventually the outside was painted black and white and down lighters were positioned to light the whole of the front of the hotel; we could now be seen from a good distance.

The second year was going to be the biggest test for us both.

The Blue Peter Hotel Badge

My First Flight as a Goose Guide

October the 22nd 1998 I had my first ever shooting group, a party of eight guns who had booked for the goose shooting, two days of rough shooting plus duck flights in the evening. This meant the bedrooms were full and the group would have their breakfast and evening meals at the hotel; they would also enjoy their nights in the bar with the locals.

It was with nervous anticipation I met the group, lads from Northern Ireland who were very familiar with the area. They had been coming over from Ireland for many years but without much success. I was certainly going to be put to the test but when dealing with wild creatures, as you know, nothing is certain and never guaranteed.

They came over by ferry arriving on the Wednesday afternoon at Stranraer where I met them personally and took them back to the hotel. What a jovial bunch of lads they were and it could be felt very clearly that they were there for a good time. Eight lads in two four by fours with a dog trailer hitched to each of them and four gundogs in each trailer. When we arrived at the hotel and the dogs had been kennelled it was time to check in. Jaqui always made a welcome pack of sandwiches and coffee on arrival giving them a chance to settle in. Then it was a visit downstairs to the bar for a beer and a chat with regard to the itinerary for the next three days. It was one of my rules that if the group were shooting that evening they would only have one drink before going out but they could have as many as they liked afterwards.

Every group who came to shoot, fish or golf was so similar, they had saved most of the year to enjoy their break away. They, as well as us, made every effort to make sure it would be good fun and everyone had an enjoyable time; we loved their excitement and anticipation and we always enjoyed meeting new people.

The itinerary for the group was a duck flight that evening followed by an early morning goose flight the next day. After breakfast they would be going on a rough shoot and then an evening duck flight. It would be the same the following day, a goose flight, more rough shooting, another duck flight in the evening before departing Saturday lunch time for Ireland. Oh, and in-between I forgot to add, they always enjoyed a tipple or three, usually far too much. It was always the same pattern, (just the same as we used to do). Looking from the business side we benefited from the full package. We were paid for the accommodation and meals, the bar and for the shooting; it couldn't get better than that. After a large evening meal the groups were usually tired and didn't bother to go into Stranraer, they loved joining in with the locals. What's the old adage, 'Bums on seats'. The income from the shooting parties alone meant I could re-invest in the future. I could develop and increase the numbers of pheasants and ducks I reared and released. I already had eight fantastic ponds for the ducks which geese also frequented very regularly but to have one or two more would mean I could give some a rest.

I had been in touch with a few of my farmers and were told there were a good number of geese going into fields near a place called Palnure; I decided that would be a good area to take the Irish lads next morning. Palnure is a good forty minutes plus south of the hotel and as I didn't have a clue what time the geese would arrive I had to get the lads up early the next morning and get them in place in good time.

That evenings duck flight went very well and the lads had a long, long evening at the bar and managed to crawl to bed at about one thirty am. They had thoroughly enjoyed their night as had the locals who had realised they could stay after hours if the guests paid for their drinks. I thought there might be a few poorly heads next day but I managed to get them up in good time and they all appeared in good spirits. After a cuppa and some toast it was all systems go to get them to Palnure in good time. It wasn't the best of mornings; not a breath of wind but once the hides and decoys had been positioned it wasn't very long before the first Pinks began to arrive.

Eight guys in four hides split into two areas of the field worked very well indeed. I didn't know until later that two of the lads had never shot a goose before. That, I thought, would be a good entry for my shooting record book. They finished with a bag of twenty two before I stopped them shooting and they were more than happy with the result. I didn't allow big bags as I wanted to be fair to the geese and not punish them too much. It was one of my rules which I always stuck to and everyone was informed about the bag limit when they booked.

I always rang Jaqui when the flight had ended so she could have breakfast prepared for them when they returned back to the hotel. It was usually between ten thirty and eleven o'clock when they finished breakfast and that was perfect timing to go out rough shooting for a few hours. There were always a few deep yawns after a very late night, an early morning and full English breakfast, it began to catch up on them, they were shattered.

Without Jaqui and my son, Simon getting involved and helping me with feeding the ponds and looking after the pheasants I simply could not have done it? Over the season it did take its toll, I became extremely tired running the bar until the early hours then getting up early to make sure the guns were up and ready, but I loved doing it and the way of life was just amazing.

The lads left on Saturday morning with plenty of geese, pheasants and ducks and had already re booked for the following year. I was now getting repeat business, something I was trying my hardest to achieve and it's always great to get the same groups coming back year after year; you make some amazing friends.

I was extremely happy, delighted in fact, my first ever shoot as a guide could not have gone better.

That's No Lady

Does it ever go wrong? Yes it does and it did occasionally. For ninety five percent of the time the shooting groups were fantastic, until one particular group came to shoot; it became a nightmare.

It was another party of eight guns wanting three full days shooting, everything including geese, ducks and rough shooting and again, for us it was a great income. They came from down south; I cannot remember exactly where they came from and they didn't arrive until early evening. I was behind the bar, busy with my village regulars on a domino evening; we had two domino teams one played at home the other away so it was always pretty busy. Once Jaqui had checked in the group they came downstairs to have a chat with me. The first question was always the same; "are there any geese in Mike"? I often teased them a little and said "They were here but have moved now and you're too late" which made a few faces fall until I told them I was only teasing and there were plenty.

When the locals had gone and the bar was closed I sat with them and went through the format for the next morning. This group had one lad who was getting a bit mouthy with me and when I spoke he would come back at me with a sarcastic reply. The others in the group seemed very uncomfortable in his presence but I didn't react and sent them off to bed ready for an early start, so far so good, Mr Mouthy had gone to sleep.

I had arranged for my friend the gamekeeper from Ardwell to let the group have a shot at some geese feeding on a few fields on the estate. This would give my geese a rest for a while and allow them to settle back in. We met up with him at the pre-arranged place and duly went about getting everything set up when Mr Mouth started criticising, quite loudly, everything we were doing. I pulled their group leader to one side and asked him what was going on and told him if it continued we would cancel the shooting for that morning. Chris the organiser of the party told me that one of the lads had dropped out just a day before because he was full of flu and this guy had taken his place.

Apart from one in the group the others knew very little about him. Chris had also felt uneasy about his attitude and had been getting a number of complaints from the others. I went over and pulled Mr Mouth to one side and told him straight, if he continued with the criticism and attitude we would be going back to the hotel and charged the full price of a goose flight. Boy, oh boy did he react and call me all the names under the sun. The atmosphere was becoming increasingly awkward. Chris grabbed him and marched him away and I could see him having words; he didn't let the guy out of his sight all morning.

All went quiet and the Greylags came in well to the decoys, everyone shot geese, all except one person, guess who? Mr Mouth wasn't at all impressed, even though he had been given plenty of chances and completely missed everything in front of him.

The flight finished and it was back to the hotel for breakfast, I could hear Mr Mouth still chuntering under his breath. The atmosphere was now making the other lads very embarrassed and once back at the hotel I had another word with Chris who promised me it wouldn't happen again. The others in the group were thinking of sending them home as it was spoiling it for the group. I said, "Them"? Apparently two had travelled together in their Land Rover and were pals of the lad who had flu. I now had two guns who could be troublesome; it was something I could do without.

The afternoon rough shoot set off really well, there were plenty of Pheasants and Woodcock and quite a few were shot including a few big brown hares.

One of the walks was through thick gorse bushes and I had to keep asking the same two lads to come back into line. They would insist on walking far too fast and far too much in front of the other guns, making it very dangerous indeed. They thought it very funny and able to do what they wanted so I cancelled the shoot on the grounds of safety and sent them all back to the hotel.

Chris was furious and I could hear one hell of a row going on in their bedroom and the language used was very explicit indeed. Chris brought them both to see me and they apologised profusely, stating it would never happen again, so a quick hand shake and that was it over and dealt with. It was now time for a much needed coffee before going out for a flight on the ducks.

The flight went well and quite a few Mallard and Widgeon succumbed to their guns but Mr Mouth had missed everything, yet again. He did, however, leave the pond laughing for once and had a good banter with the rest of the group instead of moaning all the time. The atmosphere seemed more settled which made me feel much easier but unbeknown to me there was more still to come, the night was young and the bar wasn't open yet.

Because we were a small sporting breaks hotel in a small village the groups would occasionally nip into town for a few beers, simply for a change of scenery. This was great as I could then catch up on things and not be under as much pressure to keep them entertained. All the groups were told that if they went into town they must be back to the hotel by midnight, if not the doors would be locked and alarmed. (We fibbed and said it was for insurance purposes.) No-one ever had a problem with this and once back they could always have a drink in the hotel bar.

It was about eleven forty five when they returned to the hotel by taxis. They had enjoyed themselves in a few bars in Stranraer. They said they'd had a good night and preferred to go to bed rather than have any more drink, they'd all had enough for one night plus they had to be up very early in the morning for the goose flight.

I was actually quite relieved; this meant I could have a reasonably early night. I tided the bar and was about to retire upstairs to enjoy some long needed rest when I heard a woman's voice; giggling and laughing coming out of one of the bedrooms. I pushed the door open and there sat on the bed was a young girl she was absolutely hammered and showing next week's washing very openly. I pointed towards her and shouted. GET OUT!!!! Get out now, before I call the police. Of course Mr Mouth had to have his pennyworth, "you can't speak to a lady like that". I replied angrily; "get your stuff, all of you, you're leaving the hotel NOW and she's no lady". I will give you five minutes and then I WILL call the police. I escorted the girl downstairs and out through the front door. As I turned around Mr Mouth was behind me ready to have another go at me. I quickly pinned him to the wall by his neck, warning him not to even think about trying anything. I then threw him and his friend out onto the street. The pair of them were absolutely hammered and had also been drinking more spirits in the bedroom.

Jaqui gathered their belongings together and put them outside the hotel door. Mr Mouth kept coming back shouting abuse and asking for their guns. I told them that they wouldn't get them back until the morning and not until they were sober. The police had been called and they arrested them. The idiots were sat in the car with the engine running; they were breathalysed on the spot which would mean a hefty fine and a driving ban. The police came over to find out what had happened and after my explanation took their guns away and gave the lads a cell for the night; it served them right and I hope they confiscated their guns as a lesson.

I still took the other lads out the next morning and they had a fantastic time but were very apologetic about what had happened earlier. Without those two idiots the remainder of their holiday went very well indeed and they re-booked for the following year but only on one condition!!! They didn't bring the other two back with them. It certainly was a lesson learned but in fairness nothing like that ever happened again;

it only needs one bad apple to spoil it for the rest of the group. I dread to think what might have happened. We always insisted on locking guns in the gun cabinets after a day's shooting. I hope the police threw them out of the cells very early the next morning as it was freezing and I would also like to think they lost their shot gun licences for being such stupid plonkers.

Palnure

Palnure is an area south east of the hotel on the A75 just through Newton Stewart, heading South towards Carlisle. I had permission to shoot on two very large farms and it offered superb inland goose shooting but not until late November, early December when the geese would arrive in massive numbers. The river Cree ran along the boundary for a few miles and offered plenty of duck shooting early in the season and sometimes in October Greylags would drop into the area and follow the river. I took smaller groups on a few duck flights and they had some superb Widgeon and Mallard flighting with the occasional Golden Eye and Pintail following the river, especially when the incoming tide would push them further inland.

It was an area well known for Pinks and as they flew from the Solway marsh they would head inland and later in the season they would feed regularly on the stubble fields I rented. It was all flat farmland and after heavy rainfall the geese would always come into the large flashes of water on the stubble. The only problem was they were hard to get close to. Any

A Wild Goose Chase

form of hide erected would be easily seen and spook them before coming in to land.

Palnure offered some great goose shooting, especially for the smaller groups. It's also pointless taking smaller groups out underneath thousands of geese as they could achieve their bag limit in a very short space of time. It also meant these areas had a rest from being shot and the geese could settle back in, ready for the next larger group of guns.

For me to go goose spotting on a regular basis was out of the question because of the distance and time involved. I had, therefore, arranged with the farmer at Palnure to call me when the geese were feeding on his land as it was a bit of a trek to take guns down for nothing and knowing when the geese were in was a godsend.

Everything went well and the farmer kept his word and always updated me regularly. He was another person who I got on well with and over the years we became great friends. He would make sure the parking places were ready for us in the farmyard and always came out to meet and great everyone, no matter what time it was. I remember one time in particular when one of the guns had fallen into a dyke and was soaked to the skin. The farmer kindly offered his bathroom to them to get dried and changed into clean clothing, nothing was too much trouble for him; mind you I was paying him a good figure for rent.

I hadn't been shooting very long on that farm when another, nearby, farmer called me and asked if I would be interested in letting his land for shooting. It was just across the road and wasn't big acreage, probably only a few hundred acres. Simon and I decided it was still worth looking at. It had a small river that was part tidal with very deep banks and would be a great place to take just a couple of guns for a walk about for a few hours. There was also the possibility of an early or evening duck flight up the river. Plus it meant I could see first-hand if there were any geese feeding on the other farmer's fields. It certainly had its advantages so I took it on not knowing if it would produce anything.

Geese couldn't and wouldn't feed on his land as it was surrounded by a forest and the fields were small and grass only, he didn't have any stubble. But I sensed it would be worth it and I was right. It was a jewel in the crown for me for small shooting parties and it produced quite a lot of pheasants and a great variation of ducks throughout the season.

I had arranged for the farmer's son to look after the feeders I had placed on his land, many of them in the high rushes which followed the banks on that small river. Because it had deep banks it was ideal cover to sneak up on the unsuspecting ducks, which happened many times, especially in severe weather. That farm was a gem.

A Wild Goose Chase

Walking through the rushes following the river bed produced lots of pheasants; I was drawing lots of wild birds in but I suspected there was a Pheasant shoot somewhere nearby. (Ooops!). It was an amazing area for working dogs and they loved it and of course the shooters loved working them. Anyone who shot at Palnure always asked if they could go back, year after year. I must have been doing something right, amazing scenery to enjoy, especially on warm sunny afternoons and great company or was it those all too easy ducks.

It was early October when a small group, two adults and two young boys booked in for a walk about on pheasants and possibly a couple of flights on the ducks. I thought Palnure would be ideal for a few hours walkabout and I would most likely take them on the second day as I would take them more locally for their first days shooting. The party consisted of two brothers and their two nephews, all very, very, well-spoken. The boys were aged around ten or eleven and equipped with single barrel .410. The uncles had promised them a shooting experience.

After dinner on their first night the uncles told me that that the boys were safe guns but hadn't had much experience in shooting live game. They asked if I would be willing to teach them, I must admit I was a little perturbed but everyone has to start somewhere so I engaged the help of my son Simon.

The next day we went out on one of my local farms and as we were walking along we flushed three pheasants which ran into some rushes trying to hide and get away from us. This was an opportunity to give the boy's their first lesson and have a shot at live game.

Simon and I showed them how to line up, I was on the outside of the line with both boys to my right and Simon was in the line separating the two men from the boys. We walked into the rushes very slowly and in fairness kept the line perfectly straight until a Blackbird flushed and flew towards me and flew over my head. Out of the corner of my eye I could see one of the lads swinging his gun behind the line towards me; I dropped to the floor like a brick. The shot went off right above me, if I'd remained standing, well, I dread to think what would or could have happened. The air was blue as I gave him such a bollocking, I cancelled the rest of that afternoon immediately and we returned to the hotel. They certainly weren't as safe as was suggested earlier by uncle

Once back in the hotel the eldest of the two brothers asked to speak to me in private and boy, oh boy, did he go to town on me with regard to how I had spoken to his nephew. I certainly wasn't going to take that sort of flak from anyone; I could have been killed. I put him in his place very quickly and told him that if he wanted to stay for the three days shooting he'd booked, things would have to change. He quickly calmed down and became very apologetic and asked if they could still have a duck flight that evening. On one condition I replied. "I will sit behind you, for the sake of safety". He laughed and said that would be fine.

The duck flight was a great success with plenty of Mallard, Widgeon and Teal coming in, lots and lots of shooting; they all shot but hit nothing, not even a feather was disturbed. They must have had in the region of fifty plus shots between them. They were not very experienced at all and as I was watched over their shoulders, it was obvious they were nowhere near the targets.

That evening I suggested we go to Palnure the next morning and Simon would release a few clays for them to have a practice. It would give me a chance to watch and work out why they were all shooting so badly. I wasn't too keen on taking them out rough shooting until I had seen just how they shot the clays; and I was right to be a little worried. The eldest of the two brothers had ten shots at single clays and didn't hit one; the other three were the same; not one clay was hit. They had no idea how to mount a gun, or how much lead was required, they were in fact complete novices. We actually had a very interesting and enjoyable morning teaching the group how to shoot. It was soon mid-afternoon. I asked the older brother if I could try his side by side, he handed it over and I DUSTED five pairs of clays going away from me. It was then as I was opening the gun to re-load I noticed the number 2 inlaid in gold on the rib with Purdey engraved also on the rib.

For years I had dreamt of owning a Purdey and now I was actually shooting with one and would you believe it, he had the number 1 gun back at the hotel. A matched pair of Purdeys, they must have been worth thousands. The closest I ever got to a Purdey was naming my Golden Labrador after the gun.

We addressed each and every issue they had and by the time we finished clay busting they were mounting and shooting much, much, better. In fact the younger brother was hitting well over fifty percent now. They practiced on driven, crossing and rising Teal and were finding it easier and were really enjoying themselves. Dam, if I'd played my cards right I might have got a cheap pair of Purdys. (Smiles)

It was a hard three days with them but in the end they all shot birds so it was a mission accomplished and as they left I received a fifty pound tip from each of the brothers; they'd had a fantastic time. Personally, I was glad it was over, but also pleased they had enjoyed themselves.

It was another lesson learned, I suppose but I automatically assumed that when guns came shooting they were competent shots. Just shows how wrong you can be sometimes but another lesson well learned.

A Shocking Morning

The North wind doth blow and we will have snow. Well, that particular morning it wasn't snowing but blowing a gale with torrential horizontal rain mixed with heavy sleet and it was absolutely freezing. It had been like it for nearly a week with local floods everywhere. The water flowing down the main street was now a small river and I had to cancel one party of shooters because of the horrendous conditions. There was no chance of shooting and it was forecasted for a further few days.

One of the local goose guides had booked four guns to stay with us and he wanted me to give him a hand if that awful weather ever subsided. The group had arrived by ferry from Northern Ireland and their crossing was one of the roughest that they had every experienced. They checked in and sat having a couple of beers and sandwiches in the warmth of the public bar. They were waiting for the guide to arrive and of course chatting about the adverse conditions. I tried explaining that they may have had a wasted trip but they would have none of it. They were very insistent and said they would go out no matter what.

The guide arrived and we sat chatting mainly about the severe weather conditions but trying not to deflate the group too much as they had travelled a long way. It wasn't looking very promising at all and the forecast was bleak; the conditions were not going to improve over the next couple of days.

The guide said he would give me a call next morning at five o'clock to let me know if there was a chance the group could shoot. If there was a break in the weather conditions he would take the boys onto a small loch, approximately half a mile from the hotel. They would set up the hides and put out the decoys and hope that the geese would fly even in such poor weather conditions; that was the best he could offer.

That night the boys were entertained by a few of my locals who had ventured out for a few beers. The wind was still howling and it was as if every window in the hotel was rattling; it wasn't easing in the slightest. The rain was lashing against the lower windows and doors with such intensity it was difficult to hear a normal conversation. I have never experienced wind and rain like it.

I was up before the call next morning and knew instantly that the weather wasn't any better. The Irish lads were also up and raring to go. I had a brief conversation with the guide and we decided to give it a go anyway; but it would be very doubtful anything would move in such adverse conditions, all accept us of course. What is that saying "mad dogs and Englishmen". But in this case it was Irishmen.

We geared up and set off in near impossible conditions, the vehicles being pushed and blown dramatically by such heavy winds. When we arrived at the loch I helped the guide pin down some of the decoys as it was virtually impossible to keep them on the ground in that amount of wind. I told one of the lads, Pat, to put his hide up in the corner of the field against the hedgerow as it would help protect him from the wind and driving rain. The guide took the other three lads lower down the field towards the edge of the loch. He told me that there was a stone built hide we could retreat to if the weather turned really nasty and if it became far too much for us where we were.

I headed towards the corner to see how Pat was getting on putting up his hide in such windy conditions. He kept jumping in the air shouting very loudly 'bejasus; bejasus' and kept looking back into his hide before sitting down again and then shooting straight back up into the air yet again shouting loudly once more, 'bejasus'. What on earth was he doing, what very strange behaviour. By the time I reached him I was soaked, water was running down my back and my feet were

A Wild Goose Chase

squelching. The rain was coming down so heavily I wondered just how long we could manage to endure it.

I eventually reached the hide and asked Pat what was wrong, shouting and jumping up and down like a jack in a box. He looked at me very bewildered and couldn't understand what was going on. He told me that every time he sat down and leaned back something gave him a large whack, pushing him back onto his feet forcing him to shout out loudly.

When I investigated I found that he had erected his hide around a live electric fence and because there was so much water on the ground every time he sat down he got the full force of an electric shock. Well, I got the giggles and for the life of me I couldn't stop. Every time I looked at him I would start off all over again, it was highly amusing and could only happen in 'comedy of errors'. I suggested we leave it well alone, I wasn't going to touch it, I wasn't that stupid and we went to join the others lower down the field near the loch.

Close to the loch was a natural hole that had been made into a really good hide and had a low stone wall surrounding it, a bit like a grouse butt? We were now well sheltered from the wind and driving rain. Pat had a very strong Irish accent and at times I hadn't a clue what he was saying but we were both seeing the funny side regarding that electric fence, it could only happen to an Irish man.

I was taken by surprise when Pat took a shot at something behind me and I heard a heavy splash into the water. When I looked around he had shot a Mallard which wasn't on the list, we were only there to shoot the geese. "Pat what on earth are you doing." I shouted at him loudly, "you know its geese only" Before I could say another word he was wading out into the loch in a pair of wellies to retrieve his prize. I shouted loudly for him to stop but against the wind it was impossible for him to hear me. I yelled as loudly as I could but he just kept going. Suddenly he disappeared, he went completely under the water, my face must have been a picture and all manner of thoughts were going through my head. Just as quickly as he had disappeared he reappeared, spluttering water out of his mouth. I could see his hat floating way but his hand was still held firmly onto the Mallard he had just shot. The loch had a very steep ledge only a few feet out and he had gone over it submerging himself instantly in at least nine feet of water. 'Oh my God' that's all I needed, firstly shocked by an electric fence now a half drowned Irishman. It was a quick departure to my car and then back to the hotel to get him dried off and warmed up. I think he brought out the cruel side of my nature as I couldn't stop laughing at him. The other lads remained with the guide for about an hour longer but never saw anything, not even seagulls committed to flying. The weather was that bad it's doubtful that any bird would attempt flying in it, even geese.

Our lounge bar looked like a 'Chinese Laundry' with clothes hanging over five clothes maids as close to the log fire as was safe, trying to get them dried out. They group stayed the night and left the following morning a little fed up but they re-booked for a few weeks' time and fingers crossed for an improvement in the weather. When they eventually came back they shot well and got some really good bags of geese and went back home to Northern Ireland like Lords of the Manor.

We had quite a number of shooters who came over from Ireland, it being a fairly short ferry crossing into Cairn Ryan or Stranraer. There was something about the Irish we loved having them to stay. They had such a good sense of humour (salt of the earth) and we had regular nights with them singing and really enjoying themselves entertaining the locals in the public bar.

Where Do I Put My Hands?

Sometimes we would join two small groups together and on this occasion it was a party of two men and a husband and wife team. They were quite happy with just a walk about doing a bit of rough shooting. It wasn't worth putting a small team under the geese and disturbing them, especially if I had a larger group booked in a few days later. We were setting off fairly early, just after breakfast and we were going to have a walk around the coast line, we might just surprise a few pheasants enjoying the sunshine. Suzy, the lady of the husband and wife team hadn't been feeling well at all and was suffering with a stonker of a headache; she suffered with debilitating migraines. Poor girl had to stay in bed with the curtains closed, take her tablets and rest; that really scuppered the mornings shooting.

By early afternoon she was feeling much better and the headache had completely gone so she and her husband jumped into the Discovery; the other two lads followed behind in their Jeep. I took them to one of my farms where we would get a superb view of the loch itself and also be able to see across to Northern Ireland; providing it was good visibility of course. The sea was the most fascinating blue colour; everyone would pass remarks on the colour and about the scenery being so beautiful and so vast with its rugged coastline and steep cliffs.

It was just a pleasure to be out on such a beautiful sunny afternoon wandering through the long grasses of the coastline trying to surprise an unsuspecting Michigan Blue Back. As if by magic one did get up but it was just a bit too far in front of the guns and it flew straight up in the air heading over the sea towards Ireland; it was going like a rocket. Blue Backs are one of the best flyers I have ever seen and this one didn't let us down.

It flew higher and higher until it was a dot in the sky when suddenly it must have realised that it was going in the wrong direction and turned back towards the mainland then dropping in a long way behind us. That was a bird for another day but he was a very wise one indeed and it did raise a lot of excitement.

Suzy and I walked together chatting at a safe distance behind the three shooters. My dog Purdy was enjoying herself flushing and presenting a few Woodcock and pheasants for the guns. A few brace were shot and because we had plenty of time I decided to walk through some of the heavy gorse areas hopefully to bag a few more birds, especially Woodcock; hard going at times but it always paid dividends.

The farm had a very large acreage and because of this I hadn't had time to install many stiles. The fences could be very precarious so it would be a firm grip, hopefully, on a firm fence post, place a leg half way up and a quick hop over the top. Of course, it had to happen when we had a lady with us. Suzy tried her best to negotiate the fence but failed. She had tried to get her leg over the top part of the fence by herself and in an instant she had slipped and lost her footing and came down a cropper onto the top strands of barbed wire, they were pinned between her legs and she was shouting for help; she was in excruciating pain. She asked her husband to help her but he just glared at her and walked away chuntering. He did absolutely nothing and left it to me to assist her and free her from the barbed wire as quickly as I could.

She put both her hands on my shoulders and pressed down to lift herself higher but the barbed wire had pierced her jeans and wouldn't move; it was well and truly embedded in her crotch area. I was left with no option but to put my hands down and try to get her free. I tried to put her at ease and make it less embarrassing for both of us by making a joke, "we really must stop meeting like this". We both smiled nervously as I put my hands down between her legs and

A Wild Goose Chase

untangled the barbed wire, as quickly as I could without hurting her any further. Her hubby didn't and couldn't have cared less and never moved to help her; he just stood back watching me struggle. What an arse he was, talk about a male chauvinist.

After that it was a slow limp back to the car for Suzy and once back at the hotel she made sure she was ok and not too badly hurt. The group were very happy with the walk about and shot some nice birds but it could have been much better if it hadn't been for the accident.

I made sure that there would not be another incident like that one and within a few weeks I had erected a great number of stiles on the farm. A valuable lesson learned and a much bigger First Aid kit to be carried in the Discovery.

Mike the author

Never Until After 10 pm

The hotel had some wonderful and interesting characters, it was the village local and although quite busy during the week it was especially busy at weekends.

It was a Saturday afternoon and Rangers and Celtic were playing football (old firm game) and the public bar was packed with their supporters. It was manic with the beer flowing and spirits lined up on every table. I was finding it extremely difficult to keep up with clean glasses on my own. Jaqui had one of her golfing parties due early afternoon and she was getting the rooms ready for their arrival; she wasn't therefore able to help me in the bar. Alcohol was being downed very quickly indeed but the up side was the till looked extremely healthy.

At times I was a little confused by some of my locals as one in particular supported Celtic and I wrongly assumed he was Catholic but later that day he told me he was a Protestant. One of the Rangers fans was a Catholic which confused me all the more as I watched them slowly drinking themselves into a very merry state whilst watching the match.

When we first opened the doors of the hotel and my first ever customer came strolling in, he walked straight up to me and asked in a very loud strong Scottish accent; "Twa paraffin's and twa diesels" I was completely baffled and asked him, "what does twa mean and what's a paraffin"? He told me that twa was two and paraffin was vodka and lemonade and of course the diesel would be a vodka and coke. So Twa meant two, I then asked him how do you say three. He stared back at me looking slightly bemused and simply said three. Where oh where had we come to? It was like learning a new language and they all spoke so quickly they were extremely hard to understand; they seemed to have a language all of their own. Galloway Irish I was told many months later.

The game was a cracker and the noise at times was deafening especially when there was a goal. Jaqui nipped down with bowls of chips and trays of sandwiches which kept them going for a while but half the food ended up on the floor because they were so pie-eyed. It was a belter of an afternoon and at half time it was a quick visit to the toilet and then back to the match again. I cannot remember the final score but when the full time whistle went it was as if someone had just pressed a magic button, the room cleared completely within a matter of minutes and they staggered home in time for their tea. Well, all expect two of them and boy were they well on their way; getting quite legless.

Billy and Sanny were two of my local customers, I left them chatting and leaning against the bar with their drinks while I washed all the glasses, swept the floor and locked the doors, to prevent any strays coming back in. Both men would have been in there sixties and they were completely hammered, so much so, they kept winding each other up even though they were the best of friends. One minute they were going to fight each other but in fairness I doubt they could have raised a fist never mind thrown a punch. The next minute they would have their arms around each other hugging and saying I love you Billy and Billy would reply I love you Sanny. Not one ounce of harm in either of them so I just left them to it while I continued cleaning up and re-stocking the bar ready for the evening.

The golfers had arrived and were upstairs, unpacking and enjoying a 'cuppa' and a chat with Jaqui. Eventually they came down to the bar to say hello and have a few drinks before going back up for their evening meal. They all sat down with a beer and looked totally bewildered but they were also a little concerned listening to and watching Billy and Sanny's shenanigans. I reassured them that it was harmless fun between friends and they were not to worry about it; Billy and Sanny probably wouldn't remember a thing next morning.

One of the golfers found it more fun than watching a soap opera and they loved trying to fathom out and decipher what was being said in a strong but slurred Scottish accent. I think Sanny and Billy were oblivious to the golfing party and continued with their antics of hugging each other one minute and then raising their fists the next, looking to fight each other.

I sat and chatted with the golfers as the entertainment continued and Jaqui came downstairs to let them know that their evening meal was ready and told me to nip upstairs to get some soup whilst I could before opening time and asked me to send Billy and Sanny home.

The golfers asked me to keep them informed with regard to Billy and Sanny. I told them I thought one of them would be going horizontal pretty soon and that I had a duty of care to send them home. By this time Billy and Sanny were sat at the bar on stools staring at their small shots of whisky, which must have been there for well over an hour. I told them NOT to move as I would be straight back down with my soup. I was only away a few minutes but when I went back into the bar Sanny was sat by himself. "Where's Billy, I asked"? After slowly lifting his head off the bar Sanny replied in a very slurred voice, gone for a run off, (a pee). I couldn't hear any sound at all coming from the gents' toilets so I rushed to see if Billy was okay

When I walked in, he was lying stretched across the urinals, full length with his face looking upwards; his lips had gone a deep blue colour. I honestly thought he was dead, I thought he had slipped and fallen, banging his head against the thick porcelain side of the urinals. I was filled with panic and shouted for Sanny to come to help me drag him out of the toilet area. Have you ever tried to lift a dead weight? It wasn't easy with Sanny hardly able to stand up, me pulling one way, Sanny pulling the other, it was extremely difficult.

Do I call for an ambulance, do I call the police, I was shouting as loudly as I could to get Jaqui's attention upstairs and to come down and help me but she must have been in the kitchen as she never replied so it was left to me and Sanny, who to be honest wasn't much help.

We dragged Billy into the bar, struggling to lift him up onto a stool, we managed to wedge him against the bar top with his arms folded for balance. I quickly went round the other side of the bar to get to the phone leaving Sanny holding Billy the best he could. I was just picking up the phone when I heard a groan coming from Billy; oh my God he's still alive. I ran quickly back round the bar, Billy, Billy, I shouted, nothing; Billy, Billy I shouted again, giving him a prod in the ribs. His

A Wild Goose Chase

head rose up very slowly and his swollen bloodshot eyes were peering at me in a fixed, blood shot stare.

After about five minutes he started to come around a little but his head was just like one of those toys you see on the back window of cars bobbing up and down, as if on a spring.

Jaqui had come down stairs looking for me and was now helping me with Billy. I went to get the car and hopefully between us we would get him into the car and safely home. His home was up the hill opposite the hotel, on a small housing scheme. I parked immediately outside the hotel and went to get him, "Billy, Billy, come on, my cars outside and I'm taking you home." He raised his head once again looking right into my eyes and said. "Can I have a wee dram before I go"? Now that's what you call a dedicated drinker; unbelievable.

We managed to get him into the car and I took him home. I left him in the car and knocked on the door to ask Sadie, his wife, to help me get him into the house. There was no answer so I had to assume she was out and it was left to me to man handle Billy out of the car, up the path and somehow get him into his sitting room. I managed to reach the door and Billy, after a fumbling couple of minutes found his key but I had a problem. I couldn't manoeuvre Billy close enough for me to put the key in the door and hold onto him at the same time. I asked him to stand still and not to move, I turned to put the key in the door. At the precise moment I heard a thud and Billy was lying on his back in amongst his much loved flower garden. I struggled to pick him up and half dragged him inside, settled him on the settee and made a hasty retreat.

He came back into the hotel on Sunday afternoon and he could only remember parts of the match with no recollection whatsoever of what had happened later that Saturday afternoon. He also told me that some hooligan had trampled over his flower garden and it was virtually ruined. When I told him what actually had happened that afternoon he thought I was winding him up. Mind you he did sit for quite a while before going back home relatively early to get his head down and very unlike Billy hardly touched his first pint, I wonder why?

Before Jaqui and I took over the hotel we decided we would not have a drink until after ten o'clock in the evening. We stuck to it and were never persuaded to change our mind. When working behind a bar you get a different perspective on things and how alcohol can affect what people do and say and how differently they act.

On a Saturday evening because it was very busy we employed bar staff to help. I would work with them until ten o'clock; my locals knew my rules and knew not to ask me to have a drink with them. They locals would be lined up at the bar

A Wild Goose Chase

and keep checking their watches. It's ten o'clock big man are you coming round to join us then? They knew very well that I would buy them all a drink as I always did on a Saturday night. After the many years we enjoyed at the hotel we still find it difficult to drink before ten o'clock and rarely touch alcohol through a day unless it's a wedding or christening but even then it hardly ever happens, and we stick mainly to soft drinks.

Although our local trade brought in a steady income and we ticked over quite nicely, without the summer golfing parties and the winter shooting parties the hotel was not sustainable and the locals wouldn't have had anywhere to socialize; they would have had to travel to Stranraer if they wanted a quiet drink.

Billy and I became quite good friends and I found out that he was a brilliant shot and had spent much of his life in the country amongst wild life and his knowledge was second to none. He helped me with many of the shooting groups who would ask him to spend the evening in the bar as their guest. That suited Billy down to the ground and he would retell the stories from his past poaching escapades, time and again. Boy oh boy could he tell a story, especially after a few drams of Grouse. The groups loved him and he certainly entertained them for a few drinks in return. Sometimes depending how much he'd had to drink he would burst into song.

I did invite Billy to join a small party of shooters one evening on the ducks to see if his skill in action surpassed his stories of how and what he used to shoot when he was younger. Well, he was true to his word, he really surprised me, he was a crack shot and hardly missed a thing.

If I was busy Billy would help me feed the birds which in turn gave me more time to get on with other things that needed to be done. Billy at times was a godsend to me and became an important part of my shooting team. His wife would always tell me not to let the shooters buy him too many drinks as she hated him going home late a little worse for wear, waking everyone up with his singing.

He was certainly a loveable, interesting character but there were many of them in the village; but that would fill another book.

I had a group of eight Irish lads staying with us for three days shooting and it was going to be their first evening flight on the ducks. Sometimes we would get the geese coming in which was a fantastic bonus for them and they all enjoyed it when it happened. But this particular night it was blowing a gale with some heavy rain showers mixed in.

Billy took six of the guns onto a large pond and had them well hidden in the hides before I took the other two lads onto my second flight pond which was only about four hundred yards away. It was a pot luck night really with it being so windy but I had released over five hundred ducks onto the ponds, so there should be some movement. I gave Billy strict instructions not to let the guns hammer the birds no matter what and to stop them shooting when they had a respectable bag. If the geese did come he was to stop them at two birds per gun then allow them to carry on with the ducks until I shouted to stop shooting. Just use your common sense, I told him.

It came in dark quite quickly and the shooting started early with barrages of shots coming regularly from Billy's group. My group were shooting well also but mainly Mallard and Widgeon, a few Teal flew over but they were too fast for them to get a shot.

Billy's pond was nonstop and after about twenty to twenty-five minutes I walked towards the road to shout over and ask him to cease shooting. He couldn't hear me as I was shouting into the wind and because of the noise from the guns. My two guns had had a terrific flight with over fifteen ducks picked. As we raced back to the other group (I wanted them to stop shooting), the shots kept ringing out continuously. I did hear some geese but had no idea if they had managed to get amongst them.

When I eventually reached Billy the group were starting to pack up and I asked him why so many shots and how they had got on? He told me that the birds came in continuously and never stopped. He was running between hides taking more cartridges to the ones who had run out. He was totally knackered and sat down trying to get his breath back and have a smoke on one of his rollies.

I picked up whatever I could and the bag was very large indeed with seventy one ducks (a mixed bag with Widgeon and Mallard and a few Teal) and seven Greylags .I would probably find more in the morning. I remember thinking that they must have shot quite a lot of my released birds but because Billy had not been able to hear me shout to stop the shooting and there was nothing I could have done to prevent it, (don't forget the walkie-talkies next time, I thought to myself, what a school boy error).

The atmosphere was buzzing and the lads were over the moon and told me that in all their years of shooting they had never experienced anything like it before and it was only their first night with lots more still to come. Of course Billy was the hero of the night charging around with shells and keeping them busy.

I did go back the next morning to pick up any birds we had missed. Surprise, surprise when I got to the ponds they were stacked with my own ducks. The previous night being so windy the ducks we shot must have come in from the sea to shelter; I was a very happy chappie indeed. I picked up four more Mallard and two more geese that morning and arrived back to the hotel before the lads had finished their breakfast. The count for the day was seventy five ducks and nine Greylags.

That evening Billy was invited to join them and he was in his element sitting amongst them drinking to his heart's content but he was their hero. It was unbelievable what they had to drink and as usual there was a good old sing song before they eventually retired to bed.

Because they had enjoyed a heavy night it was decided that a late breakfast would be in order and have an afternoon's rough shooting. They really enjoyed their afternoon and added lots of Pheasant, Woodcock, a few Snipe and Brown Hares to their bag.

The boys didn't manage the full three days; they had to call it a day after two days. They were absolutely knackered but they were over the moon so much, so they booked for the following year. When they left they gave me a very substantial tip which of course I shared with my right hand man, Billy. Well, it would come back over my bar so it was a win, win situation for me.

Towcett Estate

My friend Alan had been the Head Keeper for Towcett Estate in Cumbria for quite a number of years, controlling the vermin and also acting as security for the estate. He established a small driven pheasant shoot of about thirteen hundred birds which he released offering some excellent shooting. Rough shooting days, driven pheasant days and goose flighting were offered at a more reasonable price than most estates, especially for groups who would like the experience without breaking the bank. Shooting has always been an expensive hobby, as I know only too well.

Over a few years as the shoot became more established it became very popular indeed and quite a number of groups sadly could not be catered for. It was decided, because of the number of enquiries, to offer goose shooting for guns to enjoy the experience of inland shooting. On one area of the estate geese would fly in very regularly, just before dusk, to feed for an hour or two. After that they would return to the nearby waters to roost. It would be nothing like a morning flight but a good opportunity to give it a trial.

After quite a few discussions and deliberations with Alan it was suggested that a group of six guns would be an acceptable number with a bag limit of four birds each, per flight and if any Canadas came with the Greylags then five birds could be taken without adding to the bag limit of the Greylags. This meant if all went well and according to plan the guns could have a total of twenty nine geese in the bag per flight; (Twenty four Greylags and five Canadas).

I made a few calls and asked a few shooters I'd known for a long time, (wild fowlers) if they fancied a flight one evening and without any hesitation they booked. My son Simon was also going to join them and make up the number to six in total; it would be his first ever goose flight on the Greylags at evening time. The lads were also bringing a friend to pick up for them.

The estate was more than a little apprehensive because no-one had ever done it before, we would just have to wait and see if it came off. Alan had been watching the geese for a few evenings and everything was looking good with well over two thousand Greylags coming in for a late feed. They were arriving in small family groups but were sometimes joined by much larger groups of birds with a few Canadas tagging along in amongst the skeins.

Alan had placed the hides ready for the evening flight and the conditions were perfect with a slight breeze blowing in the

A Wild Goose Chase

right direction for the geese to come into the decoys and not fly around a number of times before landing.

The lads arrived on time and set out about eighty decoys. Alan sent them to their allocated hides which were placed on the fence line; the lads covered the camo nets with barley straw making them virtually impossible to be seen. I sat a good way off tucked under the fence line with my camera hoping to get some reasonable video footage of our first ever goose flight. I borrowed Alan's full stealth suit and was virtually invisible; I didn't want to spook any geese that came in.

As the evening light faded the wind dropped it was now a waiting game. Alan was at the top of a large stubble field on a higher field, a good distance away, watching through his binoculars. It can be a very long wait sometimes and we were starting to wonder if the geese were coming at all. Alan always gave me a running commentary on the radio about what was or wasn't happening but at long last he told me what I wanted to hear. "Geese are coming about a mile away in front of you." I let the lads know and then got my camera ready, making sure I was still well concealed and I wasn't going to spoil the flight for them. It has to be said that when you hear that first distant sound from the geese, every hair stands up on your body with pure excitement. The groups would always take the rip out of each other and the banter between them was always funny but they all knew the score and soon as they were in their hides the mood changed and they became responsible shots. Although, I have known grown men fall out over who shot what and argue over the silliest of things when involved with goose shooting.

It made a pleasant change for me just to sit back and let them get on with it.

The first group of birds went to our right and followed the line of the nearby wood ignoring us completely, flying low and fast. The second skein came from the same direction, again following the edge of the wood but they turned and headed straight towards us, obviously seeing the decoys set out in the field. Their wings were set as they glided quietly down the field making very little noise and rather than commit themselves immediately, they decided to take another swing before coming in but that meant the guns could get a crack at the birds flying over them. As they got a bit closer, calling loudly they weren't too sure and sensed something wasn't quite right but by then they were over the heads of the waiting guns and four birds were taken out in a volley of shots.

Within minutes more birds could be seen in the distance heading our way but the first big bunch that had followed the wood line was now making their return approach to come in from behind us. Some small groups were going across the field and had been disturbed by the sound of the guns being fired. The birds that were coming in from behind had heard the same gun fire and changed direction, flying off in a clambering panic and it was very doubtful they would return that evening. They had wiffled down from a great height and were so close to coming in but that's the way shooting can and will go sometimes.

Two more skeins went towards and over the hides but for some reason the guns refused to shoot, they certainly seemed no higher than the ones they had shot earlier. Maybe they were waiting to see if more birds would come into the decoys and closer for the two lads who hadn't yet shot.

The next birds did exactly the same and no-one shot; it became obvious that they were selecting the range at which to shoot. Skein after skein was now in the air all calling very excitably as they were looking for their buddies and wanting to get in to feed.

A few skeins had joined together and as sure as clockwork went right over the guns. There were plenty of shots now and birds were dropping all over. A line of geese followed and another high bird succumbed to two shots. The flight had well and truly started with geese in all directions, the shouting making the lad's heads turn like the heads of owls, turning and twisting rapidly, trying to locate the next bird.

A Wild Goose Chase

All went quiet for at least fifteen minutes and the sky was empty of geese so the lads quickly picked up the dead birds before any more came catching them out in the open. The group were shooting really well and even though some geese were slightly higher than normal they were hitting them. Things were going well and one lad had already reached his bag limit of four birds.

Two small groups of geese, about a field away were responding to the decoys and were dropping in like bricks when shots went off, geese had come in from behind, feet tucked up, wings set and going straight to the other two lads. Two more birds were taken. The other two small groups of geese veered of slightly but went over the top hide and a superb shot took out another goose; fantastic shooting.

Some of the geese were sensing or seeing something and decided not to come anywhere near us and for whatever reason, turned at a low altitude, and headed back towards the wood line. It was very frustrating but the birds could have seen one of the dogs or maybe someone's face; who knows but something wasn't quite right. They were not going to commit themselves anymore. A bunch of about ten birds swung over me very low but extremely fast, turned and went over their hides only to be missed by four consecutive shots.

Sheldon's group on the Greylags

There was a pattern emerging and most skeins followed it by flying from left to right and then following the wood line closely before turning into the wind and making their way down towards us. The next birds did exactly the same and went over two of the hides and I heard the sound of Canadas mixed in amongst them. Another four birds were taken. The next bunch of geese followed the same flight line but these birds were much lower and as they went over my head I could hear their wings rattling in the air. Another four down and added to the bag.

A Wild Goose Chase

Quite a few of the birds were flying much higher by now and weren't coming anywhere near us, probably because there were still some dead birds on the field, I was videoing another small bunch of about eight birds which were very high when two fast consecutive shots rang out and a bird dropped like a dot out of the sky. Two more geese were taken immediately after. There was certainly some really good, accurate shooting.

If you would like to see it, go onto YouTube, search for tewka2003 and then look for Towcett Estate Goose Flight Sept 2013; timed at 8.14 minutes on the video.

Twenty two Greylags and two Canadas succumbed to that evening flight and by all standards it went really well. It was the start of our goose flighting on the estate and we have always reached the bag limit. If the harvest is gathered in by September or mid-October it's action stations as the geese find the stubble fields very quickly but to date we haven't shot them more than three times in the season. The population of geese has grown by twenty percent each year which means much more damage and fouling is being caused to farmland; they need to be controlled and balanced.

Simon had his first shots at the Greylags and pulled off two left and rights that evening. Jammy devil, or was it just superb shooting; I like to think so, a chip off the old block.

This chapter was dedicated to Howard who was one of the guns on the flight that evening.

RIP dear friend, sadly missed by many.

Seaville

It was only by chance that we found out about this farm after chatting to one of Alan's farmer friends. It came up in general conversation when we were telling him about some of the goose shooting escapades we had enjoyed together over the years. He told us that his uncle had a farm at Seaville and the geese went onto his fields during the winter months. Well, our eyes lit up and after asking him to call his uncle we were given permission to shoot.

What an opportunity but we hadn't a clue how to find his farm; we only had brief directions and limited information but we were going, no matter what. On the map it was on the English side of the Solway and in easy reach, we picked a morning and off we went on our new goose hunt.

How we found the farm, I will never know because it was so well hidden. There were lanes, turn-offs and diversions and all we had was the good old ordinance survey map, and a torch.

Alan had been given a map of the farm and the boundaries and it's always difficult on the first visit to fathom out but we did have a rough idea of where to go. Well, I do mean rough, I think we winged it. We eventually found the farm yard and managed to park up, well out of anyone's way; the last thing we wanted was the farmer looking for us at silly o'clock because he couldn't get his tractor out of the barn.

That morning was very frosty and the ground was as hard as nails, walking across it wasn't too bad and any water or muddy areas had been frozen solid. All we had to do was follow a pathway heading towards lights that were visible on the opposite side of the Solway. Easy peasy, or so we thought. Yeah right, we got lost and struggled to find the fields where we were supposed to shoot. After walking what seemed like for ever we found the sea wall and could see the salt marsh in front of us and we could already hear the geese out on the estuary. We back tracked a field and thought, what the hell, we will put our hide up next to the hedge and hope for the best. Once it broke light we should get a better understanding of the farms layout.

It was absolutely freezing as we put out the decoys and when it started to break light the temperature, as always, dropped rapidly. Every blade of grass stood up like a sentry on duty bending at times with the sheer weight of the ragging (heavy frost) on it. We put out about twenty Shell Goose decoys and

A Wild Goose Chase

were willing to sit it out and wait for the geese to arrive, we had nothing to lose.

We were sat inside the hide having a much needed cuppa when Alan whispered, "don't move, whatever you do, don't move, there are two foxes coming towards our decoys across the field from our left side." My heart went straight to my mouth and boy was it pounding. My ten bore was leaning against the side netting of the hide, loaded with three and a half inch BBs and Alan's auto was in a similar position also leaning against the side of the netting. "Not yet, he whispered again, don't move yet, they're nearly in range, coming from the left hand side of you, wait for me to say when."

"NOWWWW", he said and I grabbed my gun as quickly as I could and looked for the two foxes which were lazily walking through our decoys without a care in the world. We both shot, four rapid shots but we missed completely. Mind you those foxes didn't half get a spurt on after the shots went off; they sped off like an express train and disappeared within seconds, onto the marsh never to be seen again.

How on earth can you miss two foxes at around twenty five yards, lazily strolling just in front of you? Well, we did making the usual excuses. Maybe it was because we were so cold and stiff. That's a great excuse so let's move on a bit and forget about those foxes, (smiles) not another word please.

It was close to eight o'clock, my toes were like blocks of ice and I was as stiff as a crutch but we could hear lots of geese and it sounded like they were airborne. The estuary was waking up, different types of birds were now showing themselves and some were scooting just over the top our hide in a hurry to get inland to feed. The geese could now be seen to our right and there were thousands of them, skein after skein but they were not heading our way at all. Pinks and lots of them shouting and clambering. They knew exactly where they were going and as they lifted they increased dramatically in height. Well, they wouldn't be feeding on our field today; they were going in the wrong direction.

The flight went on for a good thirty minutes and we heard a number of shots coming from the shore, someone was having a bit of sport and must have got under them. I had just sat down and put my coffee in its clip when Alan gave me a dig in my ribs and said, "Look in front, geese and loads of them." They were so low they had to lift to get over the sea wall but they were peeling off, slightly right of us. I started calling and got a response from one skein, they came around behind us and tucked up, whiffling down, into the decoys. Why can't geese come in front, for once I chuntered to Alan trying to turn to face them and making a complete balls of it. My movements were easily spotted by the geese and they turned away and flew well out of range.

It was now getting towards the end of the flight but a few birds were still coming off the marsh but flying extremely high. It was then we spotted a few lower birds heading towards us and this time they weren't turning away. Yes, this was it. I called and they responded well, setting their wings and gliding into us shouting and clambering excitedly. We managed to shoot three of them; we had broken the ice literally on this new farm. Things were looking good and hopefully we could keep getting permission to shoot for many years to come.

I loved going to that farm and being situated on the edge of the Solway Marsh it wasn't too far away. Over the years we visited many, many times and always managed to get geese over us. Sometimes it was pot luck but sometimes it was down to expert calling to get the geese to come and look at our decoys and by then it was far too late for them to escape such good shots, ha, ha!

Me with Alan at Seaville

To shoot just one goose was always well worth the time and effort and to watch the Pinks leaving the estuary to go and feed was an amazing sight.

East Fife: Five, Forfar: Four

For many years I travelled to the Fife area to shoot and my first ever visit was one never to be forgotten. The name Fife always reminded me of football, especially when Forfar were playing East Fife. It always made me smile, especially when the results were being broadcast on a Saturday afternoon. (For those who can remember East Fife 4 : Forfar 5).

Three friends and I booked to stay with a local man who was, I suppose, a guide of some description and had been involved in goose shooting for many years. He invited us to stay in his fabulous, three bedroomed, detached property in an area which was central to some quite amazing goose shooting. He had shooting rights on a vast acreage of land and gave us permission to shoot geese; obviously we were paying him for the shooting and the accommodation. He would take us out to find the geese then leave us to it the next morning to set up and shoot; this worked very well for us and we knew we would always be on his land and not get accused of poaching. Getting up in a morning and having free run of their kitchen, making our own toast and coffee before going out was brilliant: they never once interfered.

We arrived early one evening and were shown to the bedroom, to our surprise there was a double and two single beds in the room. I remember wondering, who would be sleeping in the double bed; well you guessed it, it was me and one of the other lads who drew the short straws. I certainly wasn't too sure about it but it actually turned out to be a great laugh.

Imagine four men, getting ready for bed, down to their long johns, standing in the middle of the bedroom, giggling like school girls, at the state of us. We must have looked like the cast from 'The Beverley Hill Billy's. Oh, heck, I was starting to become worried, was my friend gay, he was single and to my knowledge never had a girlfriend? Well, I wasn't too sure so just before going to sleep I leaned over and gave him a big sloppy kiss on his cheek and said, "good night" I rolled over and went straight to sleep. I've no idea whether he slept or not.

We drove to the shore of the Tay Estuary next morning; this brought back memories of when I shot my first goose; albeit on the opposite side of the Tay. It was still as amazing as ever especially because the other lads had never seen the Tay before and to be on that shore line was magical in every way.

We set up and waited patiently the only problem we had was the temperature. It was mid-January and bitterly cold, the sub- zero temperature was getting to us all and we were finding it very difficult to keep warm, even though we were wearing numerous layers of clothing. But our patience was rewarded, lots of geese came over us and five Pinks were taken. It was a wonderful experience and the other guns thoroughly enjoyed themselves.

After breakfast we were shown an area where lots of geese had been feeding for a few days and our guide suggested we split up into teams of two and go into different areas. Two of us would stay around the same area we had shot the previous day and the other two would go a few miles away. Both parties hoping they would be lucky and get some geese.

The guy certainly knew his geese and was very knowledgeable when it came to goose shooting. It worked a dream; we shot eight geese and the other two shot ten. The birds were still coming into land as we left the field so we decided to return to the same fields the following morning.

The forecast for the next few weeks was very heavy snow coming from the North and the temperature was going to drop to around minus ten through the day. We discussed the weather forecast with the guide and it was decided we should give next morning a miss. When we awoke next morning, it had been the right decision. We weren't going anywhere, six inches of snow had fallen through the night and everywhere was gridlocked. We spent the day chilling and enjoying our host's hospitality.

We didn't move for two days and never once saw a snow plough or gritter. Any thoughts of going out to shoot the geese were long gone; we had twenty three between us and were happy with the bag. In fairness because the conditions were so severe the geese would be finding it difficult to find clear feeding grounds and there is no way my friends and I would take advantage of the situation.

The next day the roads began to clear and we made our way cautiously homewards. Beattock Moor was a bit tricky but eventually we arrived home, tired and weary. A couple of days later there was a total blanket ban on goose shooting and wildfowling in the UK. We had been lucky and gone just in time; although we were very surprised how quickly weather conditions can change plans, especially in Scotland and how easily you can become stranded.

I've wracked my brains over the years and can't remember the guy's name. Nope; and for some strange reason I lost his contact details or I would certainly have gone back to see him. I had a strange feeling that it was his last season before he and his wife retired totally.

I did try on a number of occasions to track him down him but it wasn't meant to be. It was a shame because they were a lovely family and although I went shooting in the area many times for quite a few years our paths never crossed again; unless of course, they had moved away from the area altogether.

Seaville under the Moon

Sometimes one of us would, on impulse ask the others if they fancied a moon flight on a Friday evening at Seaville. Dave Parker, a very good friend of ours, was going to join us that evening and if we stayed long enough we would also have a morning flight.

The tide was going to be a small one and wasn't expected until three o'clock in the morning. It would be fairly safe and even if there was a breeze the tide wouldn't reach us. Rather than have something to eat before we set off we decided to stop in Wigton, on our way through and grab a Chinese take away and being much civilised we stopped to eat it in a nearby lay-by.

Dave was one hell of a character and spent most of his working life at sea and travelling all over the world. For months on end he would sit on board a ship controlling a remote vehicle laying pipe lines deep on the ocean beds; He was also a very dedicated wild fowler and loved joining us at every opportunity, especially when we went to Perthshire.

A Wild Goose Chase

Dave's downfall was alcohol, he made vast amounts of money and not only worked hard but he also played hard, when he was home. It took its toll over the years and he sadly died a few years later. It was unexpected and shocked us all greatly; we had many but always fun adventures; this chapter is dedicated to him.

We arrived at Seaville safely and parked at our usual farm; from there it was quite a long but straight walk to the sea wall. It was then only a ten minute walk across the salt marsh to reach the sand. We sat and listened to try and pinpoint where the geese were roosting but it was very difficult as the geese could be heard in different directions. When we thought we knew where they were, they would then lift and move again and re-settle in a different area. It became a quite frustrating as we tried our best to formulate a plan to get amongst the roosting geese.

Dave came up with what he thought was a brilliant idea. He would walk about half a mile towards Carlisle and then walk out onto the sands for a few hundred yards heading across the Solway. We were to go to our left then walk out the same distance on the sands and remain there, quietly. Dave would fire a shot into the air once he was in place and hopefully disturb the geese enough to make them fly away from him but towards us, giving us the best possible chance of getting a shot. The conditions were absolutely perfect; we agreed to give Dave's good idea a go. The patchy cloud would help to silhouette the geese against the moon and of course we would give it our best shot.

Dave set off and we waited a while before we moved, giving him time to get in place before we walked out onto the sand. We walked for quite some time and could hear the geese to our right; Dave might just be right. We continued to walk as slowly and quietly as we could trying not to be heard or spotted by the geese. When, all of a sudden the sand started to wobble and I really mean wobble; it was like standing on a water bed. We looked at each other, nodded, and shocked and shaking we raced back to terra firma as fast as our legs could carry us; as far away as possible from the quicksand. Boy oh boy was that scary.

Alan and I were absolutely knackered by the time we got back to the edge of the marsh and it was certainly one of the worst experiences we had ever had on a marsh. It was like something from Quatermass; that old TV programme from many years ago in the 1960's, I was only young at the time and it was scary, especially at night in the dark.

The one thing we always carried with us were flares, especially when we went on a shore venture and Dave kept us supplied with them for free. Perks of his job, I suppose. Well, we waited, and waited for Dave to fire his shot or return but nothing. We were getting extremely worried for

A Wild Goose Chase

his safety, by now. He was alone on a vast area of estuary and as we had just found out, quick sand, plus the tide was due in very soon.

At least he had his compass and flares with him should he get into difficulties and require assistance; we should then see exactly where he was. Time was ticking away very quickly and we were becoming more and more concerned and still no flares to be seen.

Dave was well aware of the tide time and its height and he wasn't stupid; we found it very strange that he hadn't returned. What the hell was he up to? Knowing Dave he would have some very plausible excuse once he did return, something like I heard a few more geese further out so I went out to locate them. Well, we couldn't wait much longer before going to get help.

Another thirty minutes had passed when Alan heard a very strange noise coming from our right and asked me to be quiet and listen. What on earth were we hearing? It was a strange scraping sound and it was coming closer and closer towards us. Then we heard this little voice say, it's only me; is that you? It was Dave's oil skins rubbing together that we could hear and he suddenly appeared into sight with a big smile as usual; Alan and I breathed a massive sigh of relief. Where the hell have you been Dave, Alan asked him? We were getting close to calling the coast guard out to find you. I've been so lost he replied, sitting down and reaching for his flask.

What happened Dave, where have you been? I asked him again. And after a very deep intake of breath and another mouthful of coffee he told us. Well, I went out onto the sand as we agreed and as I was walking I was watching the distant landmarks to help keep me in the right direction. I kept watching three lights across the other side of the Solway and it was going great until someone turned the lights off. Of course, I then lost all sense of direction so I reached inside my pocket for my compass and found I'd left it in the car. I was totally confused by this time and didn't know which way to go. I walked for ages but still didn't know in which direction I was going. Just then two of the lights came back on; I had gone in the wrong direction completely but was able to retrace my steps and get back on track again. I followed the edge of the marsh back to here and here I am!

That was the one and only time we ever attempted going after roosting geese at night; looking back it was extremely stupid, utterly forbidden and deeply frowned upon by other fowlers. In those days there wasn't as many goose shooters compared to now and we certainly didn't do any harm or damage but it could have turned out differently.

Over the years the farm produced many positive flights with memorable bags and it was a pleasure being a part of it but like everything else, time and age gets the better of you and we stopped going but one of the main reasons was because of our other interest which was the Estate, it became our priority.

This is a typical 'Daverism.' We were at Alan's one evening, having a couple of drinks before going out on an early morning flight. Alan's dog was licking its bum and I said, "I wish I could do that, not meaning it literally, of course" But quick as a flash, Dave replied, "If you give it a biscuit it will probably let you."

R.I.P. Dave Parker there will never be another like you.

A Raging Torrent

It was another one of those last minute goose flights that came out of the blue one evening. After a chat with my great friend Alan and quick call to a farmer in Perthshire, Scotland we thought, why not, let's go for a morning's flight on the Pinks; by the sound of it there was plenty. The only problem we could envisage was a very nasty weather front coming in from the North West. The forecast was gale force winds and torrential rain for most of that day. Perfect for a mornings goose flight we thought and it would give Simon more experience (aged 13) with a bit of luck the wind would keep the geese low and hopefully in range for a few shots. Well, that was the plan and we would travel up in the early hours of Saturday morning, stopping on route for breakfast near Hamilton; our favourite stop over and great food.

The travel up was quite fraught with a number of accidents around the Beattock area. The awful weather conditions made driving very difficult at times and the going was slow. We eventually arrived at the farm, tired and weary at around six thirty and parked the car inside one of the barns well out of the horrendous weather. The wind was rattling the roof and the rain was hammering against the two big sliding doors of the barn.

We hoped the morning would bring with it better weather but the storm seemed to keep increasing and I didn't like the thought of being out in it for very long. After travelling such a long way we hoped we would be able to get at least a few hours before getting soaked through to the skin. That is of course if the geese would fly in such bad conditions and even if they did we had no idea when or where they would make an appearance. We decided we would hang on as long as we could inside the barn before venturing outside. It was a hellish storm with gale force north westerly winds and freezing, sleety rain driving directly at us. It was a long wait and we watched for any signs of movement through the binoculars but visibility was very limited. We could actually hear geese calling but they were a long way off; they were moving but as yet we hadn't had sight of any skeins.

We decided to venture out to try and find where the geese were likely to go to feed. I had my trusty ten bore over my shoulder and Alan was using his five shot automatic. We were well equipped with three inch and three and a half inch Magnums. I had a box of Remington three and a half inch, two and a quarter ounce BB's and a few special loads of AAA's which were two and a half ounces. Boy, could they pack a punch; they would bring down high birds at forty to fifty yards plus, very easily. I only used those on occasions where the geese might just be on the edge of the range for the BB's.

The farm where we were shooting had many slight contours and we could hear a lot of geese in the distance so we pushed forward, going slightly uphill against the driving rain and wind to get a better view. Some of the fields were very large and it took us quite some time to cover them before we could see where the geese were landing. Boy, oh boy, there were hundreds of them but they were landing just over our boundary onto a neighbours land. Maybe, just maybe we could intercept their flight line and get a crack at them.

We were soaked through to the skin already but Simon was enjoying every minute of it and I just loved watching as his excitement mounted when he saw the numbers of geese in front of us. I suppose it's my fault for giving him goose fever but what a great experience for him to have and over the years he's loved his goose shooting and would go at any, and every opportunity.

Getting close enough to intercept the geese was going to be very difficult because of the lack of cover and the size of the fields but it wouldn't be for the lack of trying. We were soaking wet, cold, and feeling miserable and disheartened. The geese approaching the field were flying very low and struggling, considerably against the wind to make their final approach before landing. Somehow, we had to get under their flight line without scaring the geese feeding on the adjacent field.

In all my years of goose shooting this was one of the most frustrating flights I had ever experienced. We simply couldn't get anywhere near them, well not close enough to intercept the birds flying towards the ones which were already feeding. After watching a few birds take off we decided to move and try to get under the flight line and hope for the best. At least we had some cover, albeit they were gates but it was cover and meant we were going to get under the flight line.

The wind was now in our favour, blowing from behind us this meant that the geese would fly into it, or slightly across it and hopefully come close enough for us to get some shots as the birds moved between fields to feed.

My first two shots at what looked like easy targets missed completely but surprisingly the sound of my shots didn't disturb the geese in the nearby fields. I simply couldn't understand how I had missed with two shots especially as I was using my ten bore. It wasn't long before another small party of geese followed the same line as they came off the field. They came well into range, just out in front of me, probably thirty five yards at the most and not that high. This time I took my time, I stood up, made sure that I had enough lead, pulled the trigger and you've guessed it, I missed with my first shot; I stayed on the same bird increasing my lead even more and missed, yet again. My frustration was now beginning to set in. I just couldn't understand what I was doing wrong, to me they should have been very easy targets and at such close range.

Alan was shooting like me, the same birds I'd had a shot at flew over him; they didn't fly any higher or deviate in any way but he also missed them. How embarrassing for us both, it was very poor shooting indeed.

Another small group of geese came in front of me, I raised my gun and pulled the trigger and followed up quickly with a second shot and hit the same bird twice, very heavily; it started to pull out. Suddenly, it began gaining height again and began gliding way out over the field then it slowly began losing altitude and falling. My son, Simon said "I will go and get it Dad", and off he went chasing after it across the field.

As I sat waiting for more geese to take off and come my way it suddenly dawned on me. Chasing after the wounded goose, Simon was heading towards the boundary. On the boundary was a dyke which always had a good depth of water in it and by now after all the heavy rain it would be in flood. I could barely see him in the distance and my heart was pounding as I shouted and shouted as loudly as I could to get him to stop and turn back. Because of the noise of the wind and rain my voice was lost and there wasn't even the slightest chance he would hear me.

I left my gun and hot footed it across the field hoping to reach him before he got anywhere near the boundary dyke but I lost sight of him altogether. All sorts went through my mind because I knew he would not give up trying to find the goose for me. If he slipped into the water he wouldn't stand a chance, it was flowing far too fast and that's the last I would see of him. I reached the boundary hoping to catch sight of him and just as I had imagined the small boundary dyke was now a raging torrent. I looked everywhere for him, my heart was in my mouth and I was struggling to catch my breath; I was really beginning to panic now. I ran as fast as my legs would carry me following that raging torrent down the next few fields. I was knackered but there was still no sign of Simon. My mind was racing and working overtime, I had to find him hoping and praying he hadn't slipped into the water chasing after the goose.

I looked everywhere and still nothing, I needed more help and ran back to Alan to get him to come and help me search for Simon. I was in a right old state by the time I got back and was breathlessly trying to tell Alan what had happened and that I needed help to find Simon. Alan, as you can imagine was as worried as me and we were just ready to set off when he turned and smiled at me and said look behind you towards the bottom of the field. There in the distance was the small but familiar shape of my son heading back towards us carrying the goose. Pheww, the relief and emotion that swept through my body was indescribable; it hit me like a steam train. I sat down shaking like a leaf; Simon looked like a drowned rat but was safe and unharmed, smiling from ear to ear bringing back that goose.

Simon explained to us that he had gone to the boundary dyke and had seen how treacherous the water looked so he kept well away from it. He had trudged quite a distance and was on the other side of a small hill out of my line of sight. He eventually found the goose and made his way back, totally oblivious to my terror-stricken, panic.

We continued shooting but kept missing the birds, over and over again, the weather didn't improve either and at one stage when I put my hand in my pocket, it was half full of water as I fumbled around finding cartridges. A soggy packet of cigarettes and a useless lighter were in the other pocket. We were cold and soaked to the skin and only managed to shoot a few geese so we decided enough was enough and we made our way back to the farm to get dried out. It was one of the most frustrating mornings ever on the geese. We blamed everything, the wind and rain, the lead and the shells we were using but the answer was simple it was just bad shooting. It was just one of those days, never to be forgotten because normally, we don't have a problem hitting the geese.

On the way home we chatted about our day and how different it could have turned out. We had gone out that morning full of optimism even though the weather was horrendous, hoping to come home with a decent bag. It could have ended in tragedy but Simon for his age was more sensible than I gave him credit for.

Sy and Alan wet through

The Long Arm of the Law

This was now my second year and the hotel was booked solid with parties wanting geese, duck flights and of course walked up Pheasant and Woodcock shooting afternoons.

A party of six guns were expected to arrive on the lunch time ferry from Ireland. I had arranged a duck flight for that evening followed by a goose flight next morning, (providing of course they were sober enough) and then a walk about in the afternoon on pheasants before going out on an evening duck and goose flight on Ardwell Estate, with my friend, John, the Keeper. I had a few geese but John's land had far more at that time so it made sense to send them to his Estate, plus it would give my geese a break and allow them to settle back in. It was looking extremely busy for me for next three days.

The group arrived and were getting settled in when I noticed they had all come in one van, a large Ford Transit and not a dog in sight. I had retired Purdy the previous year, she had

A Wild Goose Chase

done her bit and had been the best gun dog I ever owned; she was now due a long rest. I bought a fully trained black Labrador called Burleigh but was wondering if I should get someone to help me with the rough shooting, picking up and of course working their dog or dogs to help flush more birds as it was a fairly large group and they would expect to see lots of birds.

They were a very excitable group and watching them getting ready for an evening flight was a picture. All of a sudden the hotel bedrooms and lounge looked like a bomb had gone off, there was gear everywhere.

I gathered them together in the resident's lounge and went through the shooting itinerary I had lined up for them. I did, however, notice that they were all carrying five shot autos. I had a ruling regarding auto's when shooting geese and ducks, no more than three shots were allowed in the gun at any one time Game shooting was exactly the same. I also told them that if they were not sober in a morning I wouldn't take them out because it would be a safety issue. I've seen first-hand what can happen when people are still under the influence and not sober.

It's always the same pattern be it golfers or shooters. First night is party time; they drink heavily and let their hair down; really enjoying themselves because they are on holiday. The second night slows down because they are completely knackered. They need rest and sleep especially if they stay for a third night; they sit in the bar drinking very little and retire to bed long before last orders, completely shattered.

We went out that evening and I put all the guns onto a larger pond which hadn't been shot for a little over two weeks. I knew it would be a cracking flight and true to form it was. Ducks came in from every direction and their shooting, well it wasn't the best by any standard and I had noticed a few of them cheating; they were firing five shots. Their total was eight Mallard, eleven Widgeon and a couple of Teal plus one Snipe which I must admit was one hell of a high shot. For the amount of shots that were fired they should have had at least treble the amount of birds in the bag. But all in all it was a cracker of a flight but there were no geese that evening which was a great shame.

After their evening meal they all came into the public bar for a few beers and of course, my mate, Billy would be joining them later as he did with all the groups. I could set my watch by him and he was soon sitting with the lads and having a ball. He was like my entertainments manager and did a fantastic job with his singing and stories of his past shooting escapades. The lads would sing Irish folksongs, accompanied by Billy, of course. But the evenings always ended with Billy's rendition of Danny Boy, which was actually very good.

Five o'clock the next morning I got the lads out of bed with coffee, tea, fruit juice and warm toast waiting for them and in fairness they were fine and very excited to be going out on the geese for a morning flight.

We met John from Ardwell Estate and it was only a matter of minutes before the boys were in their hides and ready for the morning flight. John had set up the hides earlier and also set out a good number of decoys; now it was a waiting game. John was an amazing keeper and nothing was too much trouble for him but it had to be done right. The Estate had their rules and bag limits were imposed and if there was any silliness the flight would be stopped immediately, it was that simple.

John also had a good many flight ponds and I could book guns with him if my ponds needed a rest. We had a good working relationship and I could always rely on him to bail me out, should the need arise.

Greylags came in really well to the decoys but the shooting was rubbish, I don't know how but they all managed a goose. I know John had a bit of a chuckle at their lack of expertise and the banter he could hear coming from the hides was brilliant. He was a master at winding people up and that morning, well, it went without question and he loved doing it. When the flight was over, eight geese had been taken and the shot count, well it should have embarrassed each and every one of them. John remarked that the field should have sunk by a good few inches with the amount of lead that was on it; no steel shot in those days.

When we were on route to the hotel, I called Jaqui to prepare their breakfasts. After they'd eaten I told them to go for a quick freshen up as we were going for a few hours rough shooting on a farm called Auch Lake. They had only had one late night and one early morning and they were already showing signs of tiredness and some of them were looking quite jaded.

I joined them for breakfast and the table was buzzing about the morning's flight on the Greylags. Everybody was blaming everyone else and between them they must have put the world to rights before agreeing to disagree. During breakfast I asked them if they fancied a go at walked up Snipe because I had an area which was full of them, probably as many as two hundred at any one time and I doubted very much that they would have seen anything like it. But like all shooting it wasn't and could never be guaranteed; it could fail dismally. They were really keen to have a go and wanted a few more Pheasants, if possible and maybe a few Brown Hares to add to their bag.

I had put myself in a bit of a dilemma really because next to the large Snipe bog was a small area of Gorse and a few trees where I had placed some feeders. Should I leave it alone and bypass it completely or do I shoot it first and hope any Snipe would remain in-situ. I was quite aware that Pheasants would be in the same area but I could only push the Snipe one way. I would have to go on my gut feeling which I did once we got there.

My decision was to go for the pheasants first but not to let the lads get too close to my Snipe bog and hopefully I would push pheasants towards them at a slight angle away from the boggy area. It paid dividends with two nice flushes and some superb birds lifting straight into the air. Only two of the lads shot birds and I must admit they were cracking shots, with four birds crumpling, stone dead in flight for only six shots between them. That was a very pleasant surprise they were actually shooting much better.

This was it, the moment I had been waiting for; I lined them up with at least twenty yards between them and told them to follow my instructions implicitly. We moved slowly forward, at a snail's pace and it wasn't long before the first Snipe were seen and suddenly there was one almighty barrage of shots. It was obvious that they were using fully loaded autos with the number of shots being fired but I thought what the hell; let's just carry on, they were not fantastic shooters and wouldn't do much damage.

As soon as they shot I froze the line and got them to pick up any empty cases as quietly as possibly before sneaking forward once again. It was unbelievable the number of Snipe in that boggy field. I certainly hadn't experienced anything like it in my lifetime but it was also was a great eye opener; the sheer number of birds. This was somewhere I could take larger groups; I just wish looking back that I'd had a video camera to record it because it would have gone viral without a doubt.

At the end of the drive their pockets were bulging with empty shell cases and have a guess how many they shot? Go on, guess? Would you believe it only two Snipe and they had nearly run out of shells? In all my years of shooting I have never had a group of guns so excited after a shoot, it's very hard to put into words but love it, they surely did.

Within the next two hours and because of the lack of shells they managed to get two Woodcock, one more Pheasant and two Brown Hares before running out of cartridges completely. What a cracking afternoon it was.

When we arrived back at the farm and they were putting the guns and game into the vehicle I told them to follow me back to the hotel. I would put the kettle on and organise a snack for them before preparing for the evening flight and hopefully giving them time for a chill out or rest before going out.

When I arrived at the hotel I went into the bar, I was parched and poured myself an ice cold drink, my throat felt like 'Ghandi's flip flops.' It had been a superb afternoon, the shooting left a lot to be desired but the group had loved it and that's all that mattered.

I was just finishing my drink and wondering where the lads had got to when the phone rang. On the other end of the phone was Peter, the nearby keeper from Corsewall Estate, their land boundaries my shooting, (the Estate released many thousands of pheasants). He was shouting at me, ranting and raving, I couldn't make out what was wrong. It took me a while to calm him down; I had no idea what he was on about or what he was saying because his Scottish accent was very strong. The air was blue and he wasn't a happy chappie for some reason. Eventually after asking him to speak much more slowly and calmer it became obvious what had happened. The lads, in their wisdom, on their way back to the hotel had spotted Pheasants feeding in a field next to the road, the same field where Peter lived in a small croft, (Keepers cottage) and he was watching them from his lounge window.

The lads had got out of their vehicle, taken out their guns and started shooting at the pheasants from the roadside. Oh, My, God. He was rightfully, spiting feathers, accusing me of everything and anything he could think of. The conversation wasn't getting anywhere, it was all one-sided so I told him I would speak to lads when they returned and find out why they had done it and I promised to call him straight back.

What the hell had they done whilst on their way back to the hotel, it put me into panic mode and of course I was still completely in the dark; the bloody numpties. When they got back I took them, very quickly, into the lounge bar and wanted to know everything they had done. They couldn't see what they had done wrong. It was totally legal in Ireland to shoot pheasants from the side of the road, no matter whose land the birds were on. I didn't think it could get any worse when the Police came into the room and asked to have a chat to me in private.

The sergeant, who I knew fairly well, was not happy with me or my guests. I took him through what the lads had told me and at that point he requested the paper work with regard to their booking, what paper work would that be, I asked? The paperwork which has all the guns registered and the permits from the correct authorities, allowing them to come and shoot.

I still hadn't a clue what he was on about but then I realised and told him Ah, they're from Northern Ireland not Southern Ireland. Nope, he said, they're from Southern Ireland so I need to look at your paper work and permissions.

I was told to stay exactly where I was whilst he went to interview the lads in the other room and by now Peter the Gamekeeper and more police had arrived and all stood with me in the lounge bar. I wasn't allowed anywhere near the shooters and as you can imagine I had gone a very strange shade of white wondering how the hell I had got the booking so wrong.

About an hour later the police sergeant came through to see me and said he would be back later to arrest me and that the lads were being taken to the Stranraer police station for further questioning. He also wanted them to collect all their belongings before they left the hotel.

I was left in limbo, not knowing what was going to happen to me, it was a very serious offence. I felt sick and unable to settle, and time seemed to drag ever so slowly. All sorts went through my mind, if I was charged, I would lose my hotel licence. The hotel would have to go up for sale. I would have to cancel all the bookings and how would Jaqui and Simon manage? It was about nine o'clock before the police sergeant came back and I had visions of me being handcuffed and escorted back to the station in the back of a police car.

He came in and asked to speak to me in private whilst Jaqui looked after the bar. He said because I had nothing logged and no paper work it meant there was insufficient evidence to prosecute but he had to give me a verbal warning. He leaned over and said, "Please never do this again or I will not hesitate to arrest you, it must never happen again." He stared deeply into my eyes, frightening the living daylights out of me.

I am totally convinced to this day that he could have arrested me but for some reason he must have taken pity on me and pulled a few strings to get any charges dropped. Was it because he visited our hotel many times with the domino teams and got to know me and realised I wouldn't knowingly break the law. I will never know but I was certainly very grateful.

I know Jaqui and I had previously discussed the permissions required for foreigners to shoot in Scotland and decided not think about it until the situation arose but we both totally forgot about Southern Ireland not being part of the UK.

Someone above was certainly looking down on me that day and I can tell you it was one of the scariest things that has ever happened to me. I could have lost everything in an instant, no more hotel, no more shooting etc., and a long prison sentence.

I assume the Irish lads were sent home to Dublin on the next available ferry and I never heard from them or the police again regarding the incident. We had to stand the loss of income but considering what had happened it was the least we could do to put things right. Any further enquires that came from Ireland we always asked, if they were from northern or southern Ireland?

Phewww, what a close call that was, it was very nearly porridge for breakfast, locked up and behind bars for god knows how long.

Welcome to AOL

It was the June of our first year in the hotel and because the building was in such a bad state of repair, both inside and out we had spent much of the time re-furbishing and decorating. Every room in the hotel had a make-over, including the cellar and the toilets which were absolutely disgusting. I also built outside dog kennels and a game larder. It seemed to be never ending and as soon as one thing was sorted another one required attention. But we were both much younger and had lots of energy and took it in our stride as we wanted the hotel to become well known for its friendliness, sporting breaks and of course cleanliness and good food.

We hadn't been open long when one evening a young couple came into our public bar to check out the new owners, it was then we met Steve and Anne. Steve was quite tall guy, about six two and had a physique like a body builder with bulging biceps, not an ounce of fat on him. He introduced himself and Anne and told us they lived fairly locally, in a small village, nearby. They were a lovely well-mannered couple and told us that they were regulars who dropped in at weekends for a few beers. They admired all the work and effort we had put in to make the place clean and homely. Steve worked on a local farm but he was getting fed up with the very long hours getting up at silly o'clock to milk the cows before starting on the rest of the chores which are required daily on a farm. His ambition was to become self-employed and have his own little business, building and repairing computers as his knowledge in that area was vast.

One evening during one of our many conversations at the bar he suggested I build a website for the hotel. I was familiar with computers, I had one upstairs in the office for typing letters, emails etc. but building a website, that was a whole different ball game; I hadn't a clue.

It was suggested that one evening Anne would come and sit with Jaqui in the public bar and she would help if it got busy; she had worked behind a bar for many years plus she knew most of the locals. Steve would begin to teach me how to build a site for the hotel. Oh boy, I'm sure he hadn't a clue what he had taken on, my knowledge of the internet could have been written on the back of a postage stamp and even then there would have been plenty of room left for more info but he said was he was up for the challenge.

Cut this, paste those, bring that in and then do that and never forget to save your work or it will be lost and we would have to do it all over again. It took him a few weeks before I could do things myself without him having to give me a prompt on what the next step was. How to do a title, how to put in pictures, how to move and drag and drop text, it was never ending and for a novice like me it was mind boggling. Steve had the patience of a saint but he continued until our first site was ready to be launched. It had a home page with the history of the hotel, a page about the golfing packages and then two pages all about the shooting which would be available. Emails were set up plus all our contact details. After my in-depth lessons on website building we always managed a few beers; a thank you for all his hard work and effort.

We finally launched the site and it was the best thing we ever did. When we advertised in golfing and shooting magazines the website details were included and the bookings began to increase. It was the start of website building for me and I've done quite a few now over the years. What would have taken me months to complete (but very much doubt I would ever have done it) I can now do in a few nights. I've also created some nice sites for friends and I owe it all to Steve to whom I will be forever grateful.

Steve had also introduced me to a site called ICQ. It was a chat site but we could only use text in those days. It was worldwide and he set it up for me so we could chat to each other via the computer some nights. I set up my profile and people were then able to see that I ran a sporting breaks hotel offering shooting and golfing parties.

One evening after quiet night in the bar I thought I would go and see if Steve was online. As I loaded up the computer and waited for it to connect I sat back and listened to what seemed like space chatter as the satellites communicated to each other. Eventually there was a connection and I heard the usual female voice, "WELCOME TO AOL" and that was me, online. I loaded up the ICQ programme and was looking forward to chatting to Steve when I saw a private message flashing and waiting for me to read and respond to.

It was from a lady in Canada called Mary and she wanted to connect and chat to me about my shooting etc. I added her to my list of two people and we started communicating with each other. I was completely blown away how my text would reach her so quickly and within seconds her reply would be on my screen. We began a very long friendship and over the time she informed me that she was in the Canadian Police Force working behind the scenes as a rifle shooter, her gun was a point three zero eight calibre and she was licenced to keep the bear population under control in a certain area. It was her job to keep thousands of tourists safe; I think she was licenced to kill five bears maximum in any one year. The funniest part about it was she was only five foot and here was a lady using quite a large calibre rifle. She actually sent me a few pictures of the bears she had culled and I was amazed at the size of them, they towered way above her head.

It was late one evening and I was having my weekly chat with her when my computer started acting quite strange and it kept crashing. It went on for about two hours and I was getting very frustrated trying everything I knew to get back online but all I kept getting was,: welcome to AOL then after about three seconds I would hear a little click, followed quickly by "Goodbye" and that was it. I hated that woman's voice saying goodbye. So the next day after a very frustrating evening I decided to get Steve to take a look at it for me but he couldn't find anything wrong. Everything seemed to be working fine so it was a total mystery but at least my computer was okay.

I knew Mary had a busy work load being in the police and the time difference between us was roughly eight hours so we couldn't chat as much as we would have liked to. But I did manage to get back in touch with her a few days later; I apologised and explained what had happened. She told me that in future when I was on the computer I had to make sure that all my windows were shut before loading up ICQ. That totally baffled me and I sat wondering if that really was the problem and why I was having interference with my signal. I told her to hang on for a few minutes and said that I would be right back.

A Wild Goose Chase

It was a clammy, humid sort of night and there was a storm brewing which would have certainly cleared the air but I went round closing all the upstairs windows and placed a small desktop fan close to me to keep me cool.

Once back on my computer I told her that I had closed all the upstairs windows. Well, I think she went into meltdown and couldn't type anything back to me for ages. I sat patiently wondering what was going on until eventually I received a very long message. It was, of course, 'windows' on the computer and NOT windows in the hotel. I was so, so embarrassed and wished at that precise time that the floor would open up and swallow me. Did I really do that, yes I did but must admit I did think it a little strange that the hotel windows would interfere with the connection, what a numpty? Even today after all those years whenever I see a nature programme about bears, rushing back into my mind is the night I closed the hotel windows. What's that book called? Internet for Dummies, well I surely was one that night.

Now Skype, I phones and other gadgetry, plus being able to put videos onto sites are classed as normal now. I'm curious to what the next thirty years will bring, maybe holograms, who knows?

After we left the hotel I lost all contact with Mary and often wonder how she got on because like us all, she will be much

A Wild Goose Chase

older now, and most probably retired from the Canadian Police Force; but I still have a little smile to myself when I hear the word 'Windows'.

She was going to organise a team of shooters to come over to visit our hotel and spend a few days goose shooting and in return she was going to sort me a few days shooting the snow geese over in Canada. On top of all that she would introduce me to a few bears, wow, now that would have been something to look forward to, not to shoot them but just to see them. Anyway it didn't work out which was a shame but the early days of the internet were very interesting in deed.

Nowadays with the internet being so easy to use and things like Facebook and all the other programmes available it's amazing how many people you can get to know and who are interested in goose shooting. Videos and pictures are readily available online to watch and it may offer many people an opportunity to go goose shooting and experience it for themselves. Long may it continue?

The Finale

Over the years I have shot not only geese but driven Pheasant, Ducks, Pigeons and I have been rough shooting, wild fowling and been involved in many other types of shooting. I can look back at my goose shooting days with a smile; they were some of the most exciting, the most exhilarating and of course most memorable times.

There isn't any other shooting, in my mind, that comes close to chasing the wild goose, namely the Pink-footed Goose or the Greylag. There is a magic about early mornings, rising well before dawn and going out onto the marsh, setting up decoys for an inland flight. Knowing, all too well that I might not get a shot, or be in range or if the birds will come over me. The adrenalin begins to flow as soon as I hear the first Wink Wink of the Pinks. Every hair on my body stands up on end and I tingle with sheer excitement.

From being a solitary wild fowler in my twenties to becoming a goose guide many years later I have many, many memories; mostly good ones but a few that I would rather forget about all together. I have been very fortunate to have been involved in the shooting world and see those magnificent birds in their thousands as they set their wings and drop down out of the sky, spiralling down into the decoys. It's something that is never forgotten.

After a long evening in the bar with the shooters I would call last orders. I would then get the stiff brush and go round the bar pretending to sweep up goose feathers and empty cartridge cases because all that could be heard for hours on end was goose shooting. Excuses why they had missed or what a cracking time they were having, or what they are going to do in the morning. They must have enjoyed themselves with us because they usually re-booked for the following year.

The one person I would like to thank is my son, Simon. He has listened to my goose stories and my shooting escapades for many years and he has now become an important part of them. One evening, at a barbeque, I was telling shooting stories to some of his friends when he said to me; "Dad, why don't you write a book and share your shooting stories with others?"

Well, I do hope you have enjoyed reading my book; there are many more stories I could have written but decided to share just a few of my favourite memories.

I have put a few videos on YouTube about Goose shooting and vermin control; search for tewka2003 and enjoy.

Before I close, please remember, if geese come and you feel they are a little bit too high, don't shoot, let them fly over; leave them for another day. Lots of wounded or pricked geese suffer for a long time before eventually dying, a slow, lingering, death. Birds that are left in a field or on a mudflat, shot by someone at an extreme range and not having a dog to retrieve them; I have seen this happen far too many times by inexperienced guns. Please don't become one of them. Just sit tight and let them get as close as possible and even then when you stand up to shoot you may be surprised just how far off they still are. It's happened to me on many occasions; but if you're out with a guide he will tell you when to shoot.

Thousands going to roost

The picture shows thousands upon thousands of geese but even with that number of birds whiffling into the decoys, they can so very easily be missed. It's the adrenalin rush or sheer excitement; it can do strange things to you.

As I've already said when I started shooting many years ago, farmers used to pay me for moving the geese off their fields and I can honestly say hand on heart that I have only abused the geese on one occasion. It was in Scotland, many, many years ago and I couldn't sleep a few nights afterwards because I took advantage of a perfect situation on the geese. I was disgusted with myself for shooting far too many. After the flight I sat looking at what I had shot and pledged to myself that I'd never ever do it again and trust me I never did; after that I only took what could be used. After seeing birds lying under a hedge, left by others to rot is so disgusting; they are such wonderful birds and they travel a great distance to winter here in the UK so never abuse them, show them some respect.

Goose shooting is one of the most passionate things I have ever done and I thank everyone who has been part of my journey, without them this book could never have been written. And remember "Goose Fever" is real, I should know because now, in my mid-sixties, it still gets to me. I still feel the same intensity as I did when I was seventeen, when I hear that very distinctive call of the Pink-footed Goose; calling as it's making its way to the estuaries or lochs to roost.

I get quite sickened viewing pictures on Facebook of very large bags and I am aware it might be because someone is making their living from goose shooting. I also know geese are increasing by twenty per cent each year but is there any need to hammer them so hard because of that increase? I think not, but that is my personal opinion?

The figures shown below are impressive; the goose populations are on the increase. But my biggest worry is, as the numbers of shooters increase each year and the number of large bags increase it might have an impact on the geese in time. I may be wrong and I do hope I am but there must be a balance to protect the geese and ensure a future of shooting for our children, grandchildren, all the wildfowlers and everyone else to enjoy.

Here is a recent report from Pink-footed Goose counts 2015
The most impressive is undoubtedly the Icelandic-breeding Pink-footed Goose population has reached a new record high of over half a million birds – just over 536,000 were recorded during the October 2015 IGC count. This is a staggering jump from the 2014 census which is explained in detail in the IGC report.

Counts of Svalbard Barnacle Geese on the Solway Firth confirmed that this population has surpassed the 40,000 mark for the first time – an estimate of 41,000 birds was made in 2015/16. This is equally remarkable population recovery considering that there were fewer than 400 birds just 70 years ago. But don't forget they are a protected species.

Finally, thanks to the efforts of the counters who took part in the 2015 International Swan Census, the new estimate of the number of Icelandic Whooper Swans has reach 34,004 birds, up from 29,000 in 2010.

A Father's Advice

By Mark Hanbury Beaufoy

If a sportsman true you'd be Listen carefully to me...

❖ *Never, never let your gun pointed be at anyone.. That it may unloaded be, matters not the least to me.*

❖ *When a hedge or fence you cross though of time it cause a loss from your gun the cartridge take.*

❖ *For the greater safety's sake. If twixt you and neighbouring gun bird shall fly or beast may run; let this maxim ere be thine "Follow not across the line."*

❖ *Stops and beaters oft unseen lurk behind some leafy screen.*

❖ *Calm and steady always be "Never shoot where you can't see."*

❖ *You may kill or you may miss but at all times think this: "All the pheasants ever bred won't repay for one man dead."*

❖ *Keep your place and silent be; Game can hear, and game can see; don't be greedy, better spared is a pheasant, than one shared.*

DRY POWDER.   Mike Wells

Useful Links

Cover picture: "First In" Pink-footed Geese, by Martin Ridley
www.martinridley.com
www.facebook.com/ridley.wildlife.art

N.G.O. www.nationalgamekeepers.org.uk

B.A.S.C. https://basc.org.uk/

Malmos gun shop: http://www.malmoguns.com

Solway Calls: web page is goosecalls.co.uk Pinkfeet and Greylag calls by Eddie Nixon

My link in YouTube. Tewka2003

Some great Facebook pages: Beaters and Pickers up. Duck and Goose Shooting Scotland, UK Country Sports. Woodpigeon Shooting. Lancashire Field Sports and many more great sites available via a search.